LAMBETH PALACE.

LIFE

OF

ARCHBISHOP LAUD.

BY

JOHN N. NORTON,

RECTOR OF ASCENSION CHURCH, FRANKFORT, KY.; AUTHOR OF "FULL PROOF OF THE MINISTRY," "SHORT SERMONS," "LIFE OF BISHOP CHASE," ETC.

"This Prelate,
Though from an humble stock, undoubtedly
Was fashioned to much honor."
Henry VIII. Act. iv. S. 2.

BOSTON:
E. P. DUTTON AND COMPANY,
Church Publishers.
1864.

RIVERSIDE, CAMBRIDGE:
STEREOTYPED AND PRINTED BY H. O. HOUGHTON.

TO THE

REV. A. C. COXE, D.D.,

RECTOR OF CALVARY CHURCH, NEW YORK;

AS ONE WHO, WHILE NOT DISPOSED TO DENY LAUD'S FAULTS,

IS WILLING TO DO JUSTICE TO HIS MERITS,

This Volume

IS AFFECTIONATELY INSCRIBED.

"THE Episcopate is one; it is a whole, in which each enjoys full possession. The Church is likewise one, though she be spread abroad, and multiplies with the increase of her progeny: even as the Sun has rays many, yet one light; and a tree boughs many, yet its strength is one, seated in the deep-lodged root; and as many streams flow down from one source, though a multiplicity of waters seems to be diffused from the bountifulness of the overflowing abundance, unity is preserved in the source itself. — Part a ray of the Sun from its orb, and its unity forbids this division of light; break a bunch from the tree, once broken, it can bud no more; cut the stream from its fountain, the remnant will be dried up. Thus the Church, flooded with the light of the Lord, puts forth her rays through the whole world, with yet one light, which is spread upon all places, while its unity is not infringed. She stretches forth her branches over the universal earth, in the robes of plenty, and pours abroad her bountiful and onward streams: yet is there one head, one source, one Mother, abundant in the results of her fruitfulness."

St. CYPRIAN, translated by the Reverend Charles Thornton, in the Library of the Fathers, Oxford, MDCCCXXXIX.

ODE TO THE MEMORY OF ARCHBISHOP LAUD.

If stern reproach from age to age
  If fiercest trials borne,
And specious lies on history's page
  With epithets of scorn,
Or life laid meekly down for truth —
If such must be before, in sooth,
  The martyr's crown is won,
How well the Church may number thee
Amid that glorious company.

Thou hadst thy *faults;* but what were they
  Who branded thee with *crime;*
Who scoff'd above thy bleeding clay,
  And flung their taunts to time?
Oh! shame that those malignant jeers
Should echo yet in these far years,
  And in this distant clime:
'Tis time the sons should quench the fires
Lit up by their relentless sires.

Ay! what were they whom later days,
  Which still distain thy dust,
Have graced with epithets of praise,
  Urn, mound, and storied bust?
The men whose deeds in glory shine,
While foul dishonor blackens thine?
  Let broken faith and trust,
A murder'd King, and trampled laws,
Proclaim how holy was their cause.

Thou had'st thy faults; yet thine a heart
  Pure, honest, faithful, true,
That would not stoop to petty art,
  A universe to sue;
A soul, when fiercest tempests woke
Their wrath, that could not bend — and broke —
  All done that man might do:
When waves the sinking bark o'erwhelm
The firmest hand must yield the helm.

PREFACE.

Archbishop Laud was an unpopular man while he lived, and he has had many to speak evil of him since his death. Indeed, so bitter has been the animosity cherished against him, that those who attempt to do simple justice to his memory must expect to share in the odium which is heaped upon his name.

The writer has been anxious in this book to set forth nothing but the truth. Ten years ago he began the task, supposing that he was as well qualified then, as he would ever be, to perform it with strict impartiality. He had not advanced far, however, before he concluded to review the history and to wait yet longer, — hoping that thus his own prejudices — if he had any — might gradually be removed. Even now he does not expect to satisfy every one, but he is disposed to think, that, with all his faults, Laud deserves to be better known, — and he trusts that this volume may place his character in a more favorable light with some, while it will be likely to modify the unqualified admiration of others.

CONTENTS.

CHAPTER FIRST.

CHAPTER SECOND.

CHAPTER FIFTH.

CHAPTER SIXTH.

CHAPTER SEVENTH.

CHAPTER EIGHTH.

CHAPTER NINTH.

CHAPTER TENTH.

CHAPTER ELEVENTH.

CHAPTER TWELFTH.

CHAPTER THIRTEENTH.

CHAPTER FOURTEENTH.

CHAPTER FIFTEENTH.

CHAPTER SIXTEENTH.

LIFE

OF

ARCHBISHOP LAUD.

CHAPTER FIRST.

A mighty Drama — Impartial Verdicts seldom rendered —Different Opinions in Regard to Archbishop Laud — Reading, with its Fortifications and Ancient Glories — The old Grammar-School — William Laud, the honest Clothier — Marriage — A puny, sickly Infant, in whose Birth the World felt little Interest — Early Dedication to God — Curious Fact — A gracious Providence watches over Laud's Infant Years — He is sent to the Free School at Reading — The little Prodigy — The shrewd Schoolmaster's Prediction — Enters College — Well-deserved Compliment — Receives his Degree, and is admitted to a Fellowship.

AMONG the mightiest dramas which the world has ever witnessed, may surely be classed that revolution which, in England, for a time, prostrated the power of the Stuarts, hewed the throne down to a block, and subjected the Church to be trampled on by a party which hated its time-honored services. If we regard the high motives enlisted in this contest, the principles which were at stake, and the momentous consequences depending on its result, we must feel that it will be invested with a still increasing interest, as long as the English language shall continue to be spoken. Nearly two centuries have now elapsed since these events took place. Six generations, too, have passed away, since these busy actors "lived and moved and had their being," and we now know them only as their deeds are written on the page of history. It is surely time, therefore, that we form our estimate of these changes, unbiased by any whispers of prejudice. Yet the reality is far different. We question much whether this generation is, on the whole, more competent to form an impartial verdict, than were those whose fathers had fought for the king at Newbury, or those who rejoiced when "the man Charles Stewart," (as they contemptuously called him,) died in front of his palace at Whitehall. We still read those histories which favor our previous views, and seldom seek in the contemporaneous records of that day to discover on which side was the truth, when for the sake of principle a nation was divided, and old friends parted to meet no more, except on the field of battle under opposing banners.*

Quite as great a diversity of opinion still prevails concerning the prominent actors in this portion of English history. This remark is especially true in regard to Archbishop Laud. To trace his career with an impartial hand is a difficult task. The writer is conscious of no enthusiastic admiration for the archbishop, neither is he disposed to be unjust, in any degree, towards those who differed from him. It will be his sincere endeavor to tell a plain, unvarnished, truthful tale.

Reading, the chief town of Berkshire, was a place of some importance in English his-

* *New York Review,* vol. x, pages 257–8.

tory, and it was protected by fortifications, even in 871, when Danes and Saxons were battling for the mastery of the soil. Long before the period when we invite our readers to visit it, in imagination, it had been shorn of its ancient glories. Its abbey, once its pride and boast, was laid waste by the spoiler's hand, but some endowments yet remain to testify to the piety of earlier days. Among these was a Grammar-School for the education of youth, founded in the reign of Edward IV., to which we shall have occasion to refer again.

In this town of Reading, there lived a clothier of good repute, and of no inconsiderable property, named William Laud. His business was so extensive that he kept many looms at work on his premises, and he gave employment to a number of weavers, and other artisans. But although Mr. Laud was an honest, thriving man, yet in a kingdom where society is so strictly divided into ranks, and where princes and nobles of high degree overshadow those of humble birth, he was merely looked upon as a plain tradesman,—well enough in his place,—but no fit associate for the rich and great. He had married the widow Robinson, whose husband had also been a clothier in the same town, a man of good property, and very generally esteemed.*

On the 7th of October, 1573, a puny, sickly infant saw the light in the house of William Laud;—but while both father and mother were glad and thankful at this evidence of God's favor, the birth of the clothier's son was little heeded by the busy world, and high nobles did not deem that one of such humble origin would yet take precedence of them, and teach the world the wholesome lesson, that the distinctions

* Mrs. Laud's maiden name was Lucy Webb, a sister of Sir William Webb, who was Lord Mayor of London in 1591. By her first husband, John Robinson, she had one son and two daughters. The son was educated for a clergyman, and became a Prebendary of Westminster, and Archdeacon of Nottingham. The daughters both married well. These facts are recorded to show how little truth there was in the statement of Archbishop Laud's enemies, that his parentage was contemptibly mean and sordid.

of earth are lightly regarded in the Church of God.

The child was so extremely weak and sickly, that few thought that he could long survive. His parents resolved, however, that nothing should be wanting on their part to promote his good, and besides enjoying the most tender care and nursing, he was early dedicated to God in holy baptism, and fervent prayers were offered in his behalf. The infant received his father's name; and WILLIAM LAUD was yet destined to live in history, and in the hearts of thousands who should regard him as the champion of orthodoxy, and a martyr in the cause of truth. While it is by no means certain that a person will attain eminence in after-life merely because he is small in infancy, it has happened curiously enough that such should have been the case with more than one who have been distinguished as lights in the world. We are told concerning Sir Isaac Newton, the great astronomer, that he was so very diminutive in size, and of so perishable a shape, that he was hardly expected to outlive the day of his birth.*

A gracious Providence watched over the early years of William Laud, and in spite of natural feebleness of body, he survived his many severe attacks of illness, and was sent in due time, with his books, to the Free-School at Reading. Here he acquired the rudiments of his education, and distinguished himself by diligent application and quickness in acquiring knowledge.

The teacher of the school was very strict in his discipline, and withal a man of close observation of character; and he ventured to predict that the clothier's son was destined for no ordinary career. Indeed, he was so firmly convinced of this that he used to say to his high-spirited and ambitious pupil, "When you are a little great man, remember Reading School." William Laud was so methodical in his habits of study, and showed such activity

* Brewster's *Life of Newton,* Chapter I.

of fancy and soundness of judgment, that he was regarded almost as a prodigy, and several persons offered to advance considerable sums of money for his support while obtaining his education, so sure did they feel of his final success.

In July, 1589, when sixteen years of age, he entered at St. John's College, Oxford, as a Commoner,* where he continued to deserve the good reputation which he had brought with him from Reading School. His tutor was Dr. Buckeridge, afterwards Bishop of Rochester, — and this excellent man did much towards developing the ripening abilities of his pupil, and in encouraging him to untiring diligence.

After spending one year at College on his own resources, young Laud received a well-deserved compliment from the Mayor and Corporation of his native town, — being nominated to a scholarship in their gift, by which means he was relieved from all expense.

* For explanations of college terms peculiar to England, see the *Life of Archbishop Cranmer*, in this series.

At the end of three years, he received his degree of Bachelor of Arts, and according to the custom of the college, he was admitted to a Fellowship. This was in June, 1594.

CHAPTER SECOND.

The first Stage accomplished, but at some Sacrifice — A great Mistake which ambitious Students make — Years of Sickness — Afflictions meekly borne — Ordination — Death of Parents — The Condition of the University of Oxford at that time — The Principles upon which the Reformation had been conducted in England — The Continental Reformers less wise in this Matter — Common Bond of Sympathy against a determined Foe — The Influx of Foreign Protestants doing Harm to the English Church — A Picture drawn by an unprejudiced Biographer — Laud stands up in Defence of the ancient Principles of the Church — His Boldness makes him many Enemies — Suspected of being a Papist in Disguise — Chosen Proctor — Takes the Degree of Bachelor of Divinity — Another unpopular Movement.

THE first stage in Mr. Laud's career was now successfully accomplished; but his eminence as a scholar seems to have been gained at some sacrifice of health and strength. How many students have made the same mistake! The pale-faced, sickly youth pores over his books day and night, bolting his meals in haste, and neglecting regular exercise, his mind bent upon one object, that of reaching a high place in his class, or of preparing himself thoroughly for the profession which he has chosen. By the time he is ready to begin the real work of life his overtaxed powers give way.

For two years after receiving his Bachelor's degree, young Laud suffered severely from indisposition, and it required all his elasticity of spirit and resoluteness of purpose to keep him from yielding to gloomy despondency. In 1798 he was made Master of Arts, and was appointed Reader in Grammar for that year. At the close ot this period he was visited with severe sickness again. However grievous these afflictions were to one who felt that he had little time to spare, they were blessed to the good of his soul, and he bore up with Christian patience and resignation.

In January, 1600, Mr. Laud was ordained Deacon by Dr. Young, then Bishop of Rochester; and in April of the next year he was admitted to the holy order of priesthood by the same prelate. The few earthly ties of kindred which had bound him to Reading were by this time broken, his father having died in 1594, and his mother in 1600.

Before going on to relate some things which occurred at Oxford, it will be necessary to say a few words in regard to the condition of the university at that time.

It will be remembered by those familiar with the principles upon which the Reformation had been conducted in England, in the time of Archbishop Cranmer, and others of blessed memory, that there had been no design on the part of its leaders to tamper at all with the framework of the Church as it had come down from Apostolic days, but merely to remove the rubbish which had accumulated during the lapse of ages, and to restore the Church to its primitive purity. The Reformation on the continent, however, had proceeded upon different grounds, and the consequences had been in many respects deplorable. The divinely appointed ministry of the Church had been abandoned, and the ancient forms and ceremonies of public worship changed, or done away with, until men began to feel themselves justified in making creeds to suit their own fancies, and to usurp the sacred office of the priesthood.

Notwithstanding these wide differences between the English Reformers and those in Germany and Switzerland,—as both parties believed themselves to be engaged in a common effort to bring back gospel truth, and to root out the grievous errors of Papal Rome,—it is not strange that they should have cherished mutual sympathy and good-will, and should seek to unite their forces by friendly correspondence, and by opposing their dangerous foe. Some of the foreign Reformers were invited to England, and they brought with them their own peculiar views, and even persuaded

Cranmer to submit the Prayer-book to them, — a few points being changed to satisfy their scruples.

Indeed, in course of time, the English Church began to feel the ill effects of having yielded too much to these influences from abroad, and when Laud was ordained to the ministry, it filled him with alarm to observe the actual condition of affairs. "Oxford," remarks Mr. Le Bas, whose judgment is too well established to be affected by any party views, "bore a greater resemblance, in many respects, to a colony from Geneva, than to a seminary of Anglo-Catholic divinity." The genius of Calvin presided in the schools. The dark theory of predestination was maintained as an essential ingredient in the faith of a Christian man. The apostolic succession of bishops was treated as little better than a fable. The authority of the Church was scornfully disregarded. The very existence of a visible Church, during the long period of Papal predominance, was gravely questioned by some distinguished divines, while others maintained that it was to be sought for only in the scattered Conventicles of Berengarians, or among the Albigenses, or the Mountaineers of Piedmont, or perhaps, among the Wicliffites of England, or the Hussites of Bohemia. In short, the whole life and virtue of religion appeared to be wellnigh concentrated into one thing, — an abrupt and impetuous departure from the Church of Rome.

Now the theological studies of Laud had taught him a very different lesson. They had been prosecuted in the spirit of the Canon of 1571, which enjoined that the interpretation of Scripture should be regulated, not by a licentious exercise of private judgment, but by a strict regard to the doctrines which had been collected from Scripture by the primitive fathers of the Church.

It was remarked by Dr. Young, by whom Laud had been ordained, that his studies had not been confined to the narrow and partial systems of Geneva; but that his scheme of divinity had been raised "upon the noble foundations of the Fathers, the Councils, and the Ecclesiastical Historians." And, hence, he pronounced that, if the young man's life should be spared, he would become a fit instrument for the Church's deliverance from the trammels of every modern school, and for her restoration to the more free and comprehensive principles of the first and purest ages. The whole plan and elevation of doctrine which this course of inquiry had set before him, he found to be in strict conformity with the original scheme of the Anglican Reformation; but in many essential respects at mortal variance with the theory and the practice which then had got possession of the schools. And he was seized with a vehement desire to bring the Church of England from this state of defection back to her native principles." *

* It is somewhat remarkable that no life of Laud has been issued in this country. Some years ago,

An opportunity was soon afforded Mr. Laud for speaking in defence of the ancient purity of the Church and its distinctive principles. A benevolent lady, Mrs. May, had once left a sum of money for the maintenance of a "foundation," as it was called, providing that certain lectures in divinity should be delivered every year; the expenses of the same being furnished from this fund. In 1602, Mr. Laud was appointed to fulfil this task, — a plain evidence that his abilities as a scholar and a theologian were considered more than ordinary. He might have selected a subject which would have been agreeable to all parties, but he preferred

one of our most energetic publishing houses sent forth a series of volumes, forming a sort of popular theological library. Prominent among these were Le Bas's lives of Wicliff, Cranmer, and Luther; but although his biography of Laud was written with the same moderation as the others, it was not included in the list, and thus, so far as these publishers were concerned, the poor Archbishop was left as a target to be shot at by the enemies of the Church, and no one to say a word in his defence. It was probably considered *unpopular* to hazard the printing of the volume.

to employ this opportunity to render an important service to the Church. It was nothing to him that such a course would make him unpopular with those whose religious principles were unsettled, and who counted the Continental Protestants, with no regular ministry, quite as orthodox as the members of the Church of England, who held fast to the ancient faith. He accordingly maintained, boldly and without reservation, "the constant and perpetual visibility of the Church of Christ, derived from the Apostles to the Church of Rome, and continued in that Church, as in others of the East and South, until the Reformation."

This lecture excited a great outburst of indignation. The ultra Protestants would not listen to the idea that the Church of Rome was a branch of the Church of Christ, in any sense,—although they could hardly deny that, under a former dispensation, Judah was still the Church of God, in spite of degeneracy and wickedness.

Dr. George Abbot, Master of University College, and Dean of Winchester, (afterwards elected to the Archbishopric of Canterbury,) took the lead in expressing opposition to the views which Laud had broached, — and, as we shall discover in a future chapter, he remembered the young man's temerity for a long while afterwards. Indeed, Abbot and his party took up the impression that he must be a friend of the Pope, in disguise, and they therefore pursued him with unrelenting hatred and severity.

In 1603, Mr. Laud was chosen Proctor by the University, and he discharged the duties of the office with such activity and zeal, as to give very general satisfaction. Towards the close of the same year, he was appointed Chaplain to the Earl of Devonshire.

In July, 1604, he became a Bachelor of Divinity. It is the custom of the University, that before any of its members receive this degree, a public exercise should be read on some theological point, — and in preparing himself to discharge the duty, the young clergyman took pains to show that the storm which had been raised by his unpopular lecture had not alarmed him. He insisted very strongly upon the necessity of Baptism, and argued the question of Episcopacy with great ability, — declaring that there could be no true Church without diocesan bishops.

No points could possibly have been selected which were more distasteful to the Puritans, and to those who held views in common with them; — and Dr. Holland, Rector of Exeter College, and Regius Professor of Divinity, rose up, and called Laud to account for unchurching the foreign Protestants, — as if the truth of the young man's positions could be affected in the least by any consequences which might be supposed to result from them. No great harm, however, was done by the opposition, — and as Laud believed himself to be contending for great and important principles, he had no idea of trimming his sails to catch the popular breeze.

CHAPTER THIRD.

No private Purposes to be served — Mr. Laud is persuaded by his Patron to do a foolish and wicked Thing — The Circumstances explained — Disastrous Conclusion of the unhappy Affair — St. Stephen's Festival kept as a Fast — Sincere Repentance and Heart-felt Supplications for Pardon — Laud's Enemies make the most of his Offences — Rather too Controversial — Bowing at the Name of Jesus in the Creed — Accused of Romish Tendencies again — Leaves the University, and enters upon his Duties as a Parish Priest — Frequent Removals — Something about the English System explained.

WE are now obliged, as an unprejudiced biographer, to relate something which, if we considered Mr. Laud's reputation alone, we should gladly omit. But as we are not writing to serve any private purpose, but strictly to bring out the truth, we shall not turn aside from any difficulty of this sort which may meet us in the way. Laud had now been three years Chaplain to Charles Lord Mountjoy, the Earl of Devonshire, — a nobleman high in favor with King James I. on account of his valuable services in Ireland. By the urgent importunity of the Earl, the Chaplain was prevailed upon, contrary to his better judgment, to solemnize a marriage between him and the Lady Penelope Devereux, daughter of Walter, Earl of Essex. The circumstances which rendered it improper for him to yield to the Earl of Devonshire's request were these.

Sir C. Blount, brother of Lord Mountjoy, had in early life formed an attachment to this lady, and his affection was reciprocated. Her admirer, being only a younger son, could not expect to marry an Earl's daughter. They could only plight their troth in secret, and part. Blount went to Court, and soon, by the aid of his position and address, made his way. The lady, after a time, was wedded to Lord Rich, an austere man, but of great wealth, and it was an eligible match, as the world said. The marriage was an unhappy one; and when Lady Rich met Sir C. Blount, (now by his brother's death Lord Mountjoy, and high in the Queen's favor,) passion overcame principle, and they sinned. They met again on Mountjoy's return from the Irish war, in which he had distinguished himself, first under Lord Essex, and then as Lord-Lieutenant, which post was conferred on him in 1599. He had returned, covered with glory, having won in 1601 the great victory at Kinsale, with the loss of only twenty men; and having, in 1603, captured the Earl of Tyrone, the rebel leader, whom he brought a prisoner to England.

Honors flowed in upon the successful warrior. James I. made him a Privy Councillor, Master of the Ordnance, and Earl of Devonshire. He met, as we said, his partner in guilt, her reputation gone, and separated from her husband by decree of Court. Drawn within the range of her fascinations, he yielded to temptation, and after much persuasion induced Laud, whom he had appointed his Chaplain, to marry him to her, on St. Stephen's day, 1605.

The conclusion of the unhappy transaction was disastrous to all parties concerned. King James withdrew his favor from the Earl, and within a year, the heart-broken nobleman sank into an untimely grave.

Laud was overwhelmed with shame and remorse, and his enemies made the most of his sad offence. It is true, he might have argued in his own justification, that it was commonly taught by the Lutheran and Calvinist preachers, that after divorce had been pronounced, both the innocent and guilty party might marry again; but he knew that neither the Church of England, nor that of Rome, allowed divorce, holding that the marriage bond is indissoluble, and that neither party may marry after separation, while the other lives. But it would have looked very badly in him, the champion of Church principles, to endeavor to escape from a painful position by adopting the loose views of his adversaries. He therefore did nothing so despicable as this, but frankly confessed his sin, and humbled himself before God in penitence and prayer, entreating His forgiveness. Until the day of his death, he continued to observe the festival of St. Stephen, on which he had performed the unlawful ceremony, as a solemn fast,—and the following prayer declares the sincerity of his heart in these acts of contrition:—

"Behold thy servant, O my God, and in the bowels of thy mercy have compassion on me. Behold, I am become a reproach to thy holy name, by serving my ambition, and the sins of others, which, though I did it by the persuasion of other men, yet my own conscience did check and upbraid me in it. Lord, I beseech thee, for the mercies of Jesus Christ, enter not into judgment with me, thy servant, but hear his blood, imploring mercies for me. Neither let this marriage prove a divorcing of my soul from thy grace and favor. For much more happy had I been, if, being mindful of this day, I had suffered martyrdom, as did St. Stephen, the first of martyrs, denying that which either my less faithful friends, or less godly friends, had pressed upon me. I promised myself that the darkness would hide me. But that hope soon vanished away. Nor doth the light appear more plainly, than I, that have committed that foul offence. Even so, O Lord, it pleased thee, of thine infinite mercy, to deject me with this heavy ignominy, that I might learn to seek thy name. O Lord, how grievous is the remembrance of my sins to this very day, after so many and such reiterated prayers, poured out unto thee, from a sorrowful and afflicted spirit. Be merciful unto me. Hearken to the prayers of thy humble and dejected servant, and raise me up again, O Lord, that I may not die in my sin, but that I may live with thee hereafter; and, living, evermore rejoice in thee, through the merits and the mercies of Jesus Christ, my Lord and Saviour. Amen."

"A *brave* example," exclaims Heylyn, "of a penitent and afflicted soul; which many of us may admire, but few will imitate."

Laud felt the consequences of this grievous mistake in many ways. His own wretchedness, from the upbraidings of conscience, was very great, and his enemies made use of it to prevent him from rising in the Church, as he had before seemed so likely to do. Dr. Abbot, in particular, took a real satisfaction in harping upon the marriage of the Earl of Devonshire.

We are disposed to think that Laud acted unwisely in appearing so soon again in the character of a controversialist, as it served to keep alive angry feelings, and could accomplish little good. But it is not for us to suggest what he might better have done; our part is to record his several acts, and leave him to bear the responsibility of them. On the 21st of October, 1606, he delivered a sermon before the University, which gave serious offence to Dr. Airay, the Provost of Queen's College, — a man of austere habits, and a decided Calvinist. The Doctor had once published a work in which he attacked the ancient custom of bowing at the name of JESUS in the Creed;* a prac-

* With a few exceptions, Churchmen, both high and low, observe this time-honored custom. We commend the following sensible observations from the pen of CHARLOTTE ELIZABETH, to the careful attention of those who have any scruples on this subject: "Among the innovations that are perpetually creeping in, changing the customs and invading the institutions of our forefathers, who, after all, were perhaps a little wiser than their descendants, I am often grieved to witness the growing neglect of a most seemly and reverential observance — bowing at the name of JESUS when reciting the Creeds of our Church. One might naturally expect, that in days when infidelity rears its brazen front with impudence unparalleled, when blasphemies abound and scoffers walk on every side, insensible to rebuke, the people of Christ would wax more jealous, would become more tenacious of every badge distinguishing them as the worshippers of an

tice which he declared to be idolatrous as the worshipping of the brazen serpent.

insulted Lord. New light, however, seems to have broken in upon some of them, which I do not believe to have come from Heaven, whencesoever else it may have emanated; teaching them that now is the time to relax in those points, — the season to rob the Lord of those outward demonstrations of respect which His enemies (who have no idea of spiritual service) delight to see withdrawn from him. 'It is too Popish,' say some of these defaulters; 'It is a mere bodily exercise, which profiteth little.'

"Craving your pardon, my good friends, it is not Popish. Popery yields little honor to Jesus; — His name is not referred to in her services nearly as often as those of other mediators — His work is undervalued — His glory tarnished. He is not even once mentioned, either in the confession or the absolution of that unhappy Church. It is true, His image and that of His cross are exhibited as objects of idolatrous worship, and that *to them* a genuflection is performed; but we, when by doing reverence at the mention of His adorable name, as Jesus Christ, the Father's only Son and our Lord, we enter a solemn public protest against the blasphemies of Socinianism, no more approximate to Popish superstition, than we do when verbally acknowledging the grand doctrine of the Triune Jehovah, which the Church of Rome has never renounced. Popery is that which once was Christianity, now corrupted, defiled, and rendered void by man's traditions and commandments. Protestantism is Christianity rescued and *Reformed*, upon the perfect model of Scripture. Our beautiful Liturgy is no other than the Romish prayer-book, purged

Laud's discourse, as we have just stated, offended Dr. Airay, who chose to con-

of all that the craft and subtlety of the devil or man had introduced to pollute a pure worship; and those who object to the beautiful symbol of the liquid cross marked on the brow of the baptized, 'in token that hereafter he shall not be ashamed to confess the faith of Christ crucified, and manfully fight under his banner, against sin, the world, and the devil; and to continue Christ's faithful soldier and servant unto his life's end,' they who stiffen the neck and knee when an assembled congregation presses, as it were, into the participation of what, either as a privilege or a menace, is proclaimed to the whole universe, that at the name of Jesus every knee shall bow, are in some peril of losing a substance, in their eager grasp after a shadowy spirituality. . . . . . To deny, or indeed to curtail the homage of the body, in order to exalt that of the soul, is going against universal experience, and against the tenor of His injunctions, who knows better what is in man than man himself does. To me, I confess it is a very delightful moment of realization in regard to the privileges of Church membership, when brethren and sisters with one accord, do outward homage to the name of Him, who in taking their nature upon Him, never ceased to be God over all, blessed forever. It is very meet that flesh, which he deigned to take into communion with Deity, should with lowly and external reverence, hail God manifest in the flesh. 'Jesus Christ our Lord,' are words of mighty, of immeasurable import: The Saviour, the Anointed, *Our* Saviour, our God, the Captain of our salvation, the Head of His body, the Church, which body (at least sider it as directed against himself. He accordingly questioned the preacher very closely, and stormed a good deal; but the doctrines of the sermon were so successfully defended by its author, that his enemies were glad to hold their peace.

Dr. Abbot appears to have lost all patience at what he regarded as Laud's assurance, and openly accused him of Romish tendencies, until it was thought hardly proper to speak to so dangerous a person on the street.

It was not until his thirty-fourth year that the future Archbishop left the University, and entered upon his duties as a

in profession) are we. It was He who wore our form, who bore our griefs and carried our sorrows; who walked our earth a persecuted, afflicted man, — who hung on the cross to atone for our sins, — descended into the grave, that it might become the gate of life to us; and now, in the majesty of His eternal glory, visits our temples and hearkens to our prayers. Let those who can, deny Him the poor tribute of grateful reverence; so long as I have power to bend a muscle, my knee shall bow in deep and willing adoration at the glorious and beloved *Name of Jesus Christ*, my Lord."

parish priest. Few important particulars are recorded concerning this portion of his life. Indeed, as he had five different parishes in less than four years, it could hardly be expected that any great results would be accomplished.

His private journal merely contains brief notices of his removal from one preferment to another; although we are informed, on good authority, that almost his first act, on entering upon his duties in any parish, was to "invest twelve poor people in a constant allowance," — besides his repairing of the houses and furnishing of the churches wherever he came.

CHAPTER FOURTH.

Several Steps of Advancement briefly Noted — Something more than a shrewd Statesman and an ambitious Prelate — Glimpses of Inner Life — A great Commotion in Gloucester — Fresh Evidences of Romanism — Bishop Smith and his Foolish Vow — A Turbulent Chaplain carries on the War — King James visits Scotland — His Plans for converting the Presbyterians to a better Faith — The King finds himself mistaken —Cutting off the Rations — Articles adopted by the University of Perth — Laud returns to Oxford — Setting up an Organ in the Chapel of St. John's College — Dangerous Sickness.

IT would interest our readers very little to be told in detail the several steps in Mr. Laud's progress, from the obscurity of a rural parish until he enters upon the wider theatre of public life. Suffice it to say, that through the influence of his friend Dr. Neile, the Bishop of Rochester, his rise was gradual though slow, gaining a stall in one place, a prebend in another, an archdeaconry in another, and a deanery in a fourth, until in 1621 he was appointed to the Bishopric of St. David's. But it would be doing great injustice to him if we left it to be inferred that he was merely prompted by ambition to reach as high a point as possible in worldly distinctions, for his private note-book and his daily devotions reveal the Christian sincerity which dwelt within his breast.

While his enemies looked upon him with suspicion, as a man who would be glad to bring the Church of England under the dominion of the Pope, and whose controversial spirit must always be engaged in some fierce dispute, the ALL-SEEING ONE saw him in the closet upon his knees, pouring forth such supplications as these:

"O merciful God, Thou hast showed me much mercy, and done great things for me; and as I was returning, instead of thankfulness, I wandered out of my way from Thee into a foul and a strange path. There Thou madest me see both my folly and my weakness. Lord, make me ever see them, ever sorry for them. O Lord, for my Saviour's sake, forgive me the folly, and strengthen me against the weakness forever. Lord, forgive all my sins, and this; and make me by Thy grace Thy most true, humble, and faithful servant, all the days of my life, through Jesus Christ our Lord. Amen."

On the 26th of September, 1617, a fire broke out under the staircase near the Library of St. John's College, by which he was exposed to considerable peril. He thus refers to it in his book of private devotions.

"September 26, 1617, die Veneris. Fire and danger. O, Merciful Father, whither shall I turn, who in my going out and my coming in, have sinned against Thee? I have gone with the Prodigal into a far country. I have expended my substance, rather Thine, in riotous living. There, I perceived everything was consumed, and that I was fit for no better company than the swine, yet neither that foul life nor the famine of Thy grace made me ever think of returning to better food. Lo, Thy judgments pursue me on my return from an ill-omened journey. The fire hath seized upon the roof which shelters me, for God saw it and delayed not. 'The fire was kindled in Jacob, and sore displeasure in Israel.' My sins, I doubt not, were perilling my College and myself. For whilst I was intent upon extinguishing the flame, it almost extinguished me. Lo, Thy goodness, O Lord, snatched me from the flames. I may almost say miraculously; for whilst a friendly hand removed me perforce, the fire, hitherto pent up, leaped forth from the place where I had purposed treading. The stairs fell into the fire, and I, had I been there, must have fallen too. O sins of mine, not yet sufficiently bewailed! O mercy of God, not yet sufficiently acknowledged! O penitence, more than ever necessary to me! O grace of God, to be implored humbly and meekly. I arise, O

Father, and lo I come, with slow and faltering step, indeed, but I come and confess I have sinned against heaven and before Thee, and am no more worthy to be called Thy son. Let me be, O Lord, what Thou wilt, so long as I am Thine. Wash me in Thy Son's blood, that I may become Thine. Grant, I pray Thee, that this affright and daily remembrance of this fire may burn out the dross and remains of sin, that the better fire of love and devotion may inflame me, walking more cautiously, with love to Thy name and hatred of sin, through Jesus Christ our Lord. Amen."

Such is the picture of Laud's inner life. The world has heard much of him as a statesman, a favorite of the King and an Archbishop, but few have known him as the humble, broken-hearted man of prayer.

While Dean of Gloucester, a great disturbance was excited, because he had the communion-table removed to the east side of the church, where it properly belonged, instead of suffering it to remain in the centre of the building, and to be treated with no more respect than an ordinary piece of furniture in a dwelling-house.

This attempt at reform had been made at the request of King James, who had long been annoyed by the irregularities which prevailed in the Cathedral of Gloucester. The Bishop of that Diocese was Dr. Miles Smith, a man distinguished for his knowledge of the Hebrew, Chaldee, Syriac, and Arabic languages, and who had rendered valuable assistance in the translation of the Bible. But although holding so high an office in the English Church, he was too thoroughly imbued with Puritan principles to give countenance to anything which might be construed into an approach to the corruptions of Rome, and when Laud had succeeded in removing the communion-table to the chancel, and had corrected some other abuses, the Bishop vowed that if such *innovations* were persisted in, he would never again enter the doors of the church! Although he lived for eight years after this, he persisted in keeping his absurd resolution.

As Dr. Smith's remonstrances had proved of no avail, a Mr. White, his chaplain, a turbulent and untractable person, determined to call in the public to his rescue, and accordingly he wrote an inflammatory letter to the Chancellor of the Diocese, complaining bitterly of the proceedings of Laud. Somehow or other this letter was found by the parish clerk in the Church of St. Michael's as he was shaking the pulpit cushions and putting everything into proper order for the convenience of the sub-Dean, who was to preach there. It spread from one to another, and the ultra-Protestant spirit of the town was fired. Fancying themselves Eliases, with a mission to testify against the abominations of Popery, the good folk of Gloucester proceeded to such unseemly and riotous behavior, that the magistracy were forced to commit the most troublesome to prison, and order others to find security for good behavior. They even went so far as to request the aid of the Court of High Commission.

This promptness, and Laud's firmness, were successful. Before the year ended the tumult had subsided. The more sensible part of the citizens began to see they were no nearer Popery because they could no longer make the Holy Table a place for depositing their coats and hats. The Bishop's absence does not seem to have been regretted, and Laud's first attempt at bridling Puritanism was successful.

In 1617, King James, after an absence of thirteen years, made a visit to Scotland. One great object of the journey was, to attempt to bring its religious establishment into closer agreement with that of England. The Episcopal Church had been set up again in Scotland in 1612,* but it had

* "The Church of Christ in Scotland and the Presbyterian Kirk are two very opposite things. The

made little progress in weaning the affections of the people from the Presbyterian

former derives its authority from Christ through a succession of regularly ordained Bishops; the latter is established by act of Parliament. Now it is acknowledged by eminent lawyers, as Coke and Blackstone, that Parliament with all its powers cannot make a woman a man, nor a man a woman; and it is equally impossible for it to make that a Church of Christ which was not so antecedently. It may, to be sure, pass a law that such a religious society shall be the established *Church* of the Kingdom, but that society does not thereby become the Church of Christ in that country. The Church of Christ of this day is derived by succession from the apostolic church at Jerusalem, and there can be but one legitimate branch in each country. The grain of mustard-seed has become a stately tree, and its branches have been spread far and wide through the earth, and everybody claiming to be a branch of the parent tree must be able to show a visible and manifest connection with it. This connection is effected by means of the Episcopal succession. Where the church exists in its integrity, it can show that its present Bishops trace their descent from their predecessors, and these again from theirs, and so on backward, till they come to those blessed apostles to whom our Lord said, "As my Father hath sent me, even so send I you. Lo! I am with you always, even to the end of the world."

"Now it is remarkable that the church of Scotland does make this claim, while her Presbyterian rival does not make it, and could not make it with justice, if it so wished. It goes back about three hundred years and there stops. It cannot leap the gulf that intervenes between the days of John Calvin and the period of the system. Instead of leaving the Scottish Bishops to proceed in a quiet and prudent way, the king determined to make short work with it, and he was vain enough to suppose that his own princely wisdom and authority could readily accomplish so difficult a task. In order to encounter the shrewd Presbyterian divines who might pluck up courage to argue with him on the subject, James selected as his chaplains men of ability and learning, Laud being one of them, and proceeded to Scotland, confident of success. As might have been anticipated, the attempt proved an utter failure, and when his majesty found that argument would not prevail, he cut off the allowance which had formerly been assigned to the Presbyterian preachers out of the royal treasury. This undignified course was not altogether ineffectual, for during the next year the assembly of

Apostolic Church, nor claim for itself, with success, a local habitation and a name previously to the advent of its ingenious inventor." — *American Church Monthly*, vol. i. pp. 120, 121.

Perth adopted the following articles: 1. That the holy Communion should be received by the people kneeling; 2. That it might be privately administered, in cases of sickness; 3. That Baptism, also, might be privately administered in cases of necessity; 4. That the birth, passion, resurrection, and ascension of the Saviour, and the coming down of the Holy Ghost, should be publicly solemnized; and 5. That children above eight years of age should receive Episcopal confirmation.

On the return of the king and his attendants from Scotland, Laud proceeded directly to Oxford, where he received a cordial greeting from his friends. Another symptom of his supposed leanings towards Rome was discovered, in the fact that he was the prime mover in having an organ set up in the Chapel of St. John's College, — an evidence of Popery which has long since ceased to alarm the most rigid Protestant.

During the year 1619, in going from

London to Oxford, he was seized with a fit while halting at an inn, which very nearly put an end to his zealous labors. God, however, spared him for sorer trials yet to come.

CHAPTER FIFTH.

Delay of Laud's Consecration — Archbishop Abbot tries his Skill with a Bow — A Dreadful Accident — The Archbishop's Distress — Dr. Williams makes himself Busy in the Matter — Other Arrangements made for the Consecration of the Bishops Elect — Deplorable Condition of the Diocese of St. David's — The new Bishop begins the Work of Reform — Puritan Opposition to the Consecration of Churches — A Chapel Built at Aberguilly — Prayer at the Laying of a Corner-Stone — New Grounds of Opposition — First Visitation of his Diocese — Guarding the Entrance to the Priesthood.

WE mentioned in the last chapter, that at the close of several steps of gradual advancement, Laud was nominated as the Bishop of St. David's. His consecration was delayed for several months, by a very unfortunate circumstance which happened to Archbishop Abbot. While on a visit to Lord Zouch, at Branshill Park, in Hampshire, he was prevailed on to accompany a hunting-party to the field, and even to try his skill with a cross-bow. Being a miserable marksman he accidentally shot a man instead of a deer, — an extremely awkward incident in the life of a Bishop, to say nothing worse about it. Poor man, he was very miserable, as might readily be supposed, and it was strongly argued by many conscientious divines, that the shedding of blood, although purely accidental, disqualified a Bishop for the performance of any holy office. The Archbishop retired to Guilford to weep over his misfortune and to await the settlement of this perplexing question. Meanwhile, Dr. Williams, formerly Lord Keeper, who had an overweening anxiety to be Primate himself, determined to make the most of the accident, and wrote to the Duke of Buckingham, then the king's favorite, enlarging upon the penalties to which the Archbishop had rendered himself liable at canon and statute law, and gravely suggesting that a man who was stained with blood could not, without marked impropriety, occupy a seat so important as that of Primate and Patriarch of the English Church.

His Majesty issued a commission to the Lord Keeper Williams, the Bishops of London, Winchester, (the saintly Andrewes,) St. David's, (elect,) Exeter, (elect,) two Judges of the Common Pleas, and two Doctors of the civil law. For a long time the delegates were divided. At last the more merciful course, of which Andrewes and Dr. Martin, Dean of the Arches, were the champions, prevailed. Andrewes could not bring himself to strain obsolete canons, even to condemn a man he disliked, for what clearly might happen to any of his brethren at any time. Besides, he knew that, bad archbishop as Abbot was, Williams would be worse.

These considerations influenced him to take the side of moderate counsels, and he had the satisfaction of finding his view of the case indorsed by the great legal authority of Sir E. Coke, who, when asked if a Bishop might hunt lawfully in his own or any other's park, replied, that by law the Bishop's dogs belonged to the King at his death, and that therefore there could be no doubt but that the Bishop might use them when alive.

The Archbishop therefore escaped without any punishment inflicted; and, as we have not much which we can record to his credit, it would not be fair to omit that he ever kept the day of his misfortune as one of fasting and penitence, besides settling a pension on the widow.

But the benevolence of the King in showing favor to Archbishop Abbot, could not silence the scruples of Laud and the other Bishops elect, who were waiting for consecration; and accordingly a royal commission was directed to the Bishops of London, Chichester, Ely, Landaff, and Oxford, to discharge this sacred duty. The consecration service took place in the chapel of London House, on Sunday, November 18, 1621, when Laud was elevated to the Bishopric of St. David's, Williams to that of Lincoln, and Carey to Exeter.

Although the village of St. David's gave name to the diocese to which Laud was appointed, it was not the residence of the Bishop. The invasions of the Danes, Norwegians, and other nations, had obliged the heads of the Church, in earlier times, to seek for a quiet home in the little town of Aberguilly, near Carmarthen. At the period when Bishop Laud entered upon his duties there, the Diocese of St. David's was in a miserable condition,—more churches being required to meet the wants of the people, and the Episcopal residence fast going to ruin. Finding no chapel connected with his house at Aberguilly, he built one, which was designed not only for the use of his own family, but also for that of the inhabitants who lived around.

He thought it right and in accordance with the teachings of the Scriptures and the practice of the early Church, that a place designed for the worship of Almighty God, should be dedicated to HIM by special solemnities. The irreverent spirit of the age was not prepared for this, and again Laud was exposed to the abuse of fanatics, because, forsooth, he advocated what now seems so natural and appropriate to us, — the consecration of churches. He thus refers to the opening of his chapel, in his diary, August 28, 1625:

"I consecrated the chapel or oratory, which I had built at my own charge in my house, commonly called Aberguilly House. I named it the chapel of St. John the Baptist, in grateful remembrance of St. John's College, in Oxford, of which I had been first fellow, and afterwards president. And this I had determined to do. But another thing intervened, (of no ill omen, I hope,) of which I had never thought; it was this: On Saturday, the evening immediately preceding the consecration, while I was intent at prayer, I know not how, it came strongly into my mind that the beheading of St. John the Baptist was very near. When prayers were finished, I consulted the calendar. I found that day to fall upon Monday, to wit, the 29th of August, not upon Sunday. I could have wished it had fallen upon that same day when I consecrated the chapel. However, I was pleased that I should perform this solemn consecration at least on the eve of that festival; for upon that day His Majesty King James heard my cause about the election to the Presidentship of St. John's College, in Oxford, for three hours together, at least, and with great justice delivered me out of the hands of my powerful enemies."

The same reverential feeling which prompted the Bishop of St. David's to urge the propriety of consecrating chapels and churches, led him to insist that the first stone of a new building for the worship of God should be laid with becoming religious ceremonies.

When, towards the close of his life, he was brought to trial by his enemies, the following prayer, which had been found in his study, was produced by one of the hot-headed Puritans, as proof of his unfaithfulness to the Church of England, because a prayer of nearly the same import was contained in the Romish Pontifical:

"*At the laying of the first stone of a Chapel.*

"O Lord, merciful and gracious, these, Thy people, are preparing to build a place for Thy service. Accept, I humbly beseech Thee, their present devotion, and make them perfect, both in their present and future duty; that while Thou givest them ease to honor Thee, they may with the greater alacity go on in Thy service. And now, O Lord, I have by Thy mercy and goodness put to my hand to lay the first stone of this building; 'tis a corner-stone — make it, I beseech Thee, a happy foundation, a durable building. Let it rise up, and be made, and continue a house of prayer and devotion through all ages, that Thy people may be taught to believe in Jesus Christ, the True Corner-Stone, upon Whom they and their souls may be built safe forever. Grant this for the same Jesus Christ, our most blessed Lord and Saviour, to Whom, with the Father and the Holy Spirit, be ascribed all power, majesty, and dominion, this day and forever. Amen."

Even those who are by no means admirers of Laud, now give him credit for his efforts to restore dilapidated churches and cathedrals to their former beauty, that they might be rendered more worthy of that BEING to whom they were dedicated.

"His spirit in him strove
To cleanse and set in beauty free
The ancient shrines, mindful of Him whose love
Swept with the scourge His Father's Sanctuary.*

* *The Cathedral,* by the Rev. Isaac Williams.

Nothing can be more just than Laud's remarks on this subject before the bar of the House of Lords: "Ever since I came in place, I have labored nothing more than that the external public worship of God, so much slighted in divers parts of this kingdom, might be preserved, and that with as much decency and uniformity as might be. For I evidently saw that the public neglect of God's service in the outward face of it, and the nasty lying of many places dedicated to that service, *had almost cast a damp upon the true and inward worship of God, which, while we live in the body, needs external helps, and all little enough to keep it in any vigor.*"

Before following Laud in his career as a statesman, it will be proper to insert the brief record which has been left of his first visitation of his Diocese.

"1622. — July 5. I first entered into Wales.

"July 9. I began my first visitation at the College at Brecknock, and preached.

"July 24. I visited St. David's and preached.

"July 25, Aug. 6, 7. I visited at Carmarthen and preached. The Chancellor and my Commissioners visited at Emlyn.

"July 16, 17. And at Haverfordwest, July 19, 20.

"Aug. 15. I set forward towards England from Carmarthen.

"1622.—Feb. 9. I ordained Edmund Provant, a Scot priest. He was my first-begotten in the Lord."

The private devotions show how heavy the responsibility of laying on of hands was felt to be by Laud:

"Lord, I am now at Thy altar, at Thy work. Keep me, that I lay not my hands suddenly upon any man, lest I be partaker of other men's sins, but that I may keep myself pure in Jesus Christ our Lord. Amen. Lord, give me grace, that as oft as they shall come in my way, I may put them in remembrance whom I have ordained, that they may stir up the gift of God, which is in them, by the laying-on of my hands, through Jesus Christ our Lord. Amen."

Another entry shows that he guarded carefully entrance into the priesthood, excluding the unworthy :

"Sept. 24. One only person desired to receive Holy Orders from me, and he found to be unfit, on examination. I sent him away with an exhortation, not ordained."

CHAPTER SIXTH.

Laud takes his Seat in the House of Lords — King James finds the Commons undisposed to yield to his Wishes — He makes an Appeal to the Bishops — The famous Controversy with Fisher — The Countess of Buckingham is placed under the Tuition of the King — Long-continued Disputes, and little to show for them — Prince Charles goes to Spain — Laud appointed Chaplain to Buckingham — He suffers serious Inconvenience from his Intimacy with the Great — A Prayer which was thought very suspicious — Difficulty with Williams — Disquieting Night Visions — Archbishop Abbot once more.

THE day after his consecration, Bishop Laud took his seat in the House of Lords, the highest branch of the English Parliament. The clothier's son of Reading is making himself known, and the haughty nobles are obliged to show him deference.

The affairs of the English government

were then in a critical condition. King James was becoming impatient for a replenishment of his treasury, while the members of the House of Commons were not disposed to listen to his request unless he gave heed to their petitions and remonstrances concerning the growth of Popery. They were even prepared to advise him to declare war against Spain, and to marry his son to a lady of the Protestant faith. As soon as the king heard this, he sent a letter to the Speaker, forbidding the House to interfere with affairs of State; but he soon found that the day had passed when the monarch's word could make the people yield implicitly to his will. The Commons insisted that every member of the House should enjoy unmolested liberty of speech, and that anything which went wrong in the kingdom was a proper subject of debate. James felt that his own royal privileges were thus interfered with, and he was so indignant, that he dissolved the Parliament on the 9th of January, 1622, after it had been in session little more than a month.

The king, finding that the Commons were not disposed to help him, addressed letters to the Archbishop, and the other Prelates near London, soliciting them to exert themselves in their respective Dioceses to raise the money which he required. Laud was one of those to whom application was made, and although he had not yet visited his See, he forwarded the royal epistle to his clergy, with the request that they would attend to it.

On the 17th of February, we find him preaching at Westminster, and towards the close of the next month, at Court. The sermon which he delivered on this last occasion, he was commanded to print. But the early part of 1622 was memorable for something more important still. We refer to Laud's conference with the Jesuit Fisher. The history of the affair is as follows:

" While the sectarian spirit was busy among the middling and lower classes in this country, the genius of the church of Rome was on the wing, among the more exalted regions of society. There was much at that time to encourage the restless emissaries of the Papacy. The king was notoriously bent upon the Spanish match. His son devoted himself to the prosecution of it with a passionate and romantic ardor. And the project was urged onward by the Marquess of Buckingham, who was afterwards the prince's confidential guide and companion in the ridiculous adventure of the journey to Madrid. Under these circumstances, to win over the all but omnipotent statesman to the See of Rome, was manifestly an object well worthy of the choicest arts and resources of the school of Loyola. For, if that object were once accomplished, there could be little doubt that the Romish creed would be favored with the amplest toleration, when the Infanta of Spain should become the consort of the heir apparent. The first attempt, it was resolved, should be made upon the mother of the favorite;

and the enterprise was intrusted principally to John Perse, a Jesuit, who usually bore the name of Fisher. His success was answerable to the most sanguine wishes of his party. The illustrious lady was driven from her steadfastness; and the Jesuit was actively following up his advantage, when the matter came to the knowledge of the King. His Majesty was sorely troubled with the report of these designs and practices. For some time he took the Countess under his own especial tuition. But even the Royal Theologian was not a match for the wily Jesuit. And finding that he sped but poorly in his task, James listened to the counsels of the Lord Keeper; who, on hearing of the lady's defection, had addressed a letter to her son upon the subject, wherein the wisdom of the children of light is curiously mixed up with the wisdom of the children of this world. "Your mother," he says, "is departed out of the bosom of the Church of England. . . . . I would we could bring her home so soon, that it might not be seen she had ever wandered! . . . . It is time to let your Lordship know that the mouth of clamor is opened, that now the recusants have a potent advocate to plead for their immunity, which will increase their number. When this is banded in the high and popular Court, by the *tribunitian* orators, what a dust it will raise! . . . . My Lord, your mother must be invited, or provoked, to hear debates between learned men. . . . . Let her Ladyship have her champions with her. Let the conferences be as solemn as can be devised. The King himself ever present at the disputes, and the conflux of great persons as thick as the place will permit. Let your Lordship's industry and earnestness be conspicuous, &c. &c. &c. If her Ladyship recover of her unstableness, you have won a soul very precious to you. But, if the light within her be darkness, the notice of your Lordship's pious endeavors will fill the kingdom with a good report, and will smell to every nostril like a sweet savor. My Lord, courage, &c." *

* Le Bas's *Life of Laud*, page 55-6.

It was finally arranged that a debate should be held between the Jesuit and some competent clergyman of the English Church, — and the first person chosen for the purpose was Dr. White, Rector of St. Peter's, Cornhill, who had long been distinguished for his zeal against the Romanists. A single disputation not being sufficient, a second followed, which the King condescended to attend. Other important points being still unexamined by the controversialists, a third conference was held on the 24th of May.

From the beginning of the discussion, Laud had been constantly consulted, and he now took a more active part in it. The reputation which he had already gained for ability as a controversialist was amply sustained, and all Protestants are free to acknowledge that the Jesuit was completely demolished. The actual results of the discussion, however, do not appear to have been very great. It is true, the Countess of Buckingham seemed to be favorably impressed for a while, but she finally went back again to her Romish errors, — and as a punishment for her obstinacy, (as the King regarded it,) she was banished from the Court. The idea of attempting to make people orthodox by force is so absurd as to provoke a smile, and we should thank God, that in this respect at least the present age is an improvement on that in which the Countess lived.

So far as Laud himself was concerned, he did not gain much by his efforts in this matter. The infamous Buckingham was convinced of the claims of Protestantism, — so far as he found it convenient and politic to be so, — but his spiritual adviser, the Bishop of St. David's, incurred the bitterest hatred of the Papists, without securing the confidence or good-will of the ultra Protestants — Laud held that the Church of England occupied a middle place between Rome and Geneva, — and he could therefore have expected no sympathy or support from those of extreme views on either hand.

And here, after the conclusion of the famous controversy with the Jesuit Fisher, the visitation of the Diocese of St. David's was made which was mentioned in the last chapter.

What real sympathy could have existed between so unprincipled and wicked a man as Buckingham, and one so pure in his life, and so zealous for religion as Laud most certainly was, it is difficult to understand. The conference with Fisher brought them into close and confidential intercourse, and although the Bishop may have hoped that the King's favorite might aid him in rising to higher honors in the Church, he did not hesitate to speak plainly to the nobleman of his faults, and to recommend more serious attention to the concerns of his soul.

On the 15th of June, Buckingham appointed Laud his chaplain, and on the next day, being Trinity Sunday, he received the Holy Communion at Greenwich. This intimacy proved to be a most unfortunate one for the Bishop, as it served to fix upon him the suspicion of treacherous designs against the religion and liberties of the country.

His enemies went so far as to charge him with having encouraged the expedition of Charles and Buckingham into Spain, with the design of turning the Prince from the Protestant faith, and of securing the reëstablishment of Popery in England. All this is so absurd that it would be wasting words to attempt to disprove it.

The whole Protestant zeal of the kingdom was arrayed against the marriage of Charles with any Roman Catholic princess, and we can therefore easily understand how Laud should be regarded with suspicion from his intimate relations with Buckingham, and from the fact that he was known to have corresponded with him during his visit to Spain. The following prayer, which he daily used in behalf of Prince Charles and his companion, was afterwards brought up against him as containing language which indicated that he was playing a double part.

"O Most Merciful God and Gracious Father, the Prince hath put himself to a great adventure. I humbly beseech Thee make a way clear before him. Give Thine Angels charge over him; be with him Thyself in mercy, power, and protection, in every step of his journey, in every moment of his time, in every consultation and address for action, till Thou bring him back with safety, honor, and contentment, to do Thee service in this place.

"Bless his most trusty and faithful servant, the Lord Duke of Buckingham, that he may be diligent in service, provident in business, wise and happy in counsels, for the honor of Thy Name, the good of Thy Church, the preservation of the Prince, the contentment of the King, the satisfaction of the State. Preserve him, I humbly beseech Thee, from all envy that attends him, and bless him that his eyes may see the Prince safely delivered to the King and State, and after it, live long in happiness, to do them and Thee service, through Jesus Christ our Lord. Amen."

The part which was thought suspicious was this, — that "the way might be cleared before them, *in their great adventure*."

Our confidence in Laud's soundness as a Churchman is such that we cannot suspect him of any design to play into the hands of the Papists; and we can only deplore that his burning zeal, which might have been so usefully employed in the duties peculiar to his sacred office, should have been so often misdirected by intruding itself into the affairs of state.

Although Buckingham possessed the influence which was successfully exerted in advancing the interests of his devoted chaplain, the enemies of the latter never ceased to make war against him by secret intrigue and open opposition.

The Lord-Keeper Williams continued to be a sort of leader among them. The character of the two men was so different, that they could hardly agree on any subject. While Laud felt that the safety of the English Church depended upon her being kept uncontaminated by Puritan principles, Williams was always anxious to make concessions, and to conform as far as possible to the views of the foreign reformers.

Laud could not pursue a crooked policy, while Williams always preferred it. Laud shrunk from dissimulation, — Williams delighted in it. The unhappy difference between them is thus noticed by Laud in his Diary: —

"October 3, 1623: I was with my Lord Keeper, to whom I found some one had done me very ill offices." And similar entries occur in abundance. So great was the annoyance, that Williams even figured in his dreams, and on one occasion, he seems to have made it a special object of prayer to God, and to have experienced much consolation by recalling to mind Psalm lvi. — "The Lord is my Helper; I will not fear what man can do unto me. Who is not safe under that shield? Protect me, O Lord, my God."

Abbot, Archbishop of Canterbury, already mentioned, was another of Laud's enemies; "a man," says Clarendon, "totally ignorant of the true constitution of the Church of England, and the state and interest of the Clergy." His whole life was an evidence of this, while his utter want of forethought for his poorer brethren was shown by his treatment of a proposition which Laud made to him for the purpose of lightening the burden of taxation which fell upon the poorer clergy.

The Convocation of 1624 voted a large subsidy to the King on occasion of the rupture with Spain; but the time for levying it was limited from February 19 to March 16, 1624-5. Laud who had once been a parish priest, (which Abbot never was,) knew this would press hard upon the country clergy, and devised a plan for lightening its burden, which met with the approbation of Buckingham and Williams.

Abbot thought differently, however, and "was very angry; asked what I had to do to make any suit for the Church; told me never any Bishop attempted the like at any time, nor would any but myself have done it; that I had given the Church such a wound in speaking to any Lord of the Laity about it, as I could never make whole again; that if my Lord Duke did fully understand what I had done, he would never induce me to come near him again. I answered, I thought I had done a very good office for the Church, and so did my betters think. If his Grace thought otherwise, I was sorry I had offended him, and I hoped (being done out of a good mind, for the support of many poor vicars in the country, who must needs sink under three subsidies a year,) my error, if it were one, were pardonable. So we parted. . . . . May God bless me, his servant, laboring under the pressure of them who always wished ill to me."

CHAPTER SEVENTH.

Three Petitions made to the King, which he saw fit to grant — Bells and Bonfires — Sickness of his Grace of Buckingham — Laud not so yielding as he is thought to have been — James's Death — His Son succeeds to the Throne — State of the Kingdom — An empty Treasury and an impolitic War — The new King and his Parliament at variance — Laud looks into the Future — Puritanism in full Blossom — The Crosier and the Sceptre enter into a firm Alliance — The Commons become Theological Inquisitors — They arraign the King's Chaplain for a singular Offence — "I see a cloud arising."

ON the 19th of February, 1624, the English Parliament assembled. Three petitions were made to the King, — first, that the Spanish treaty might be dissolved, — secondly, for a war with Spain; and thirdly, that a general fast might be appointed. James granted these requests, and the Commons were so much gratified, that his own wishes in regard to a liberal appropriation of money were promptly complied with. The rupture with popish Spain was hailed with delight throughout the kingdom, and celebrated with bells and bonfires.

During the month of May, the Duke of Buckingham was attacked with a dangerous illness, and Laud, in his character of private chaplain, watched by his bedside, and did all that he could to contribute to the comfort of the sufferer. His own feeble health had taught him to sympathize with the sick, — and not only was he kind to those who had the ability to reward him for it, but he was equally attentive to the poor. We read of him, on a certain occasion, coming from Hampton Court to London, to visit one of his servants, William Pennell, "whom I left sick at home."

Although Laud was devotedly attached to his patron, it was impossible for the Duke to persuade him to do anything which he believed to be wrong.

When an effort was made to apply the

funds of the Charter House to the support of the army, and Buckingham urged him to vote for the measure as one which would greatly relieve the necessities of the King, he resolutely refused, and thus saved from spoliation a noble establishment, which has done so much for the cause of literature and benevolence.

The reign of King James was drawing to a close. He died on the 27th of March, 1625, leaving an only son, then in his twenty-fifth year, to succeed him on the throne. Hume has briefly summed up this monarch's character when he says, "that all his qualities were sullied with weakness and embellished by humanity." *

* Hume's England, Vol. IV., p. 494,—[Harpers' edition.] Although Macaulay is a very unsafe authority in all that relates to the Church, we cannot but think that his remarks in regard to the reign of James are full of truth. "Of James the First, as of John, it may be said, that if his administration had been able and splendid, it would probably have been fatal to our country, and that we owe more to his weakness and meannesses than to the wisdom and courage of much better sovereigns. He came to the throne at a critical moment. The time was fast approaching when either the

On the day of his father's death, Prince Charles was proclaimed king. Knowing as

King must become absolute, or the Parliament must control the whole executive administration. Had he been, like Henry the Fourth, like Maurice of Nassau, or like Gustavus Adolphus, a valiant, active, and politic ruler; had he put himself at the head of the Protestants of Europe; had he gained great victories over Tilly and Spinola; had he adorned Westminster with the spoils of Bavarian monasteries and Flemish cathedrals; had he hung Austrian and Castilian banners in St. Paul's, and had he found himself, after great achievements, at the head of fifty thousand troops, brave, well-disciplined, and devotedly attached to his person, the English Parliament would soon have been nothing more than a name. Happily, he was not a man to play such a part. He began his administration by putting an end to the war which had raged during many years between England and Spain, and from that time he shunned hostilities with a caution, which was proof against the insults of his neighbors and the clamors of his subjects. Not till the last year of his life could the influence of his son, his favorite, his Parliament, and his people combined, induce him to strike one feeble blow in defence of his family and of his religion. It was well for those whom he governed that he in this matter disregarded their wishes. The effect of his pacific policy was, that in his time no regular troops were needed; and that, while France, Spain, Italy, Belgium, and Germany swarmed with mercenary soldiers, the defence of our island was still confided to the militia. As the King had no standing army, and did not even attempt to form one, it would have been wise in him to avoid any conflict with his people. But such was his indiscretion, we do the sequel of his history, we cannot read unmoved the secret prayer of Laud upon the accession of the new king: "God grant to him a prosperous and happy reign."

The English Church, at the time of James' death, was apparently prosperous, although, as Heylyn expresses it, "She was beleaguered by two great enemies: assaulted openly by the Papist, on the one side, and undermined by the Puritan, on the other."

She could boast of men of great ability and learning, and of most exemplary lives, whose worth was soon to be tried in the furnace of adversity."

Popular clamor had forced James into an impolitic war, — and the same unworthy favorite who had fomented so much mischief during the reign of the father, was now to

that while he altogether neglected the means which alone could make him really absolute, he constantly put forward, in the most offensive form, claims of which none of his predecessors had ever dreamed." *

* Macaulay's History, vol. i., p. 65–6.

act as the evil genius in the affairs of the son. Charles found an empty treasury, and what was still more embarrassing, the House of Commons refused supplies for a contest which had been of their own seeking. Thus, at the very beginning of his reign, the King and Parliament were at variance.

The Commons possessed no real power or influence, long after they were recognized as one of the three estates of the realm. Even when the power of the feudal nobility had been broken, some generations elapsed before they became sensible of their strength. They had crouched at the feet of Henry VIII. Elizabeth with a high hand repressed their rising spirit; but even Elizabeth might have failed in this if her personal qualities and the uniform wisdom of her government had not imposed upon them a profound and well-deserved respect, and if the nation had not been sensible of the blessings which they enjoyed under her singularly favored reign. Under James, who was not more arbitrary in principle than he was flexible in temper, they began to feel and exercise their power; and when Charles succeeded, they were in a disposition to abuse it.

"A crisis had arrived at which it might have been possible, had there been prudence on both sides, to define and balance the Constitution without a struggle. The needful political reform might have been accomplished with less difficulty than had attended our religious reformation, because there was less evil to be corrected. Some grievances there were which cried aloud for redress, some vexations which might easily have been removed, and, in redressing them, the government would have acquired both popularity and strength. But the men by whom popular opinion was directed aimed at more than this, and Charles was surrounded by counsellors, of whom some were weak and others treacherous. He used to say it was better to be deceived than to distrust; this opinion he inherited from his father, whose maxim it was that suspicion is the disease of a tyrant.

"Charles distrusted no one so much as himself; and to that infirmity of purpose it was owing that he did not make himself an absolute king, after it was rendered impossible for him to govern as a constitutional one. He had nearly succeeded, when, having gained over to his service one of the best and ablest leaders of the popular party, he tried the experiment of governing without a parliament, and raising, by his own prerogative, the necessary revenues which the Commons had persisted in withholding. The liberties of England would then have been lost, if a stronger principle than the love of liberty had not been opposed to him." *

The first Parliament of Charles assembled on the 18th of June, 1625, on which occasion Laud preached before the King and the House of Lords.

From some passages in his sermon, he seems to have looked forward into the future almost with a prophetic eye. He knew

* Southey's *Book of the Church,* chapter XVII.

the spirit of those who longed and labored for the overthrow of the Church, and he did not hesitate to speak plainly what he thought.

"At this distance of time, we can scarcely realize what a deadly evil Puritanism was, nor the dreadful heresies to which it gave birth. What is left of it is innocent compared with the Puritanism of the time of Charles I. It was, in fact, a system of opinions which had grown up in the Church, at utter variance with its doctrines and discipline. The Church of England appealed for her justification to the early ages. Puritanism laughed antiquity to scorn. The Church limited private judgment by reception of the creeds of the undivided Church; Puritanism claimed for itself the most unbridled license, and profanely attributed to its most intemperate sallies the authority of the Spirit. The Church of England believed our Lord's words, 'Except a man be born of water and the Spirit, he cannot see the kingdom of God.' Puritanism denied the necessity or the efficacy of baptism, and reduced it to a naked sign. Confirmation was the subject of profane jesting. The Church placed prayer above preaching; Puritanism exalted preaching above prayer. The Church adhered to the necessity of Episcopal ordination; Puritanism held that any one who fancied he was called by God might lawfully serve in the sacred ministry.

"All the pious ceremonies retained by the Church were laughed at and set at nought by the Puritans. They would neither stand at the gospel, nor bow at the name of Jesus, nor receive the communion in the attitude of suppliants. They tore the altar from its position in the east, and rejoiced to see it in the body of the church, — a receptacle of hats or books. They could not endure painted glass, and shut their ears to the sweet influences of sacred music. The beautiful order of the Church's calendar had no charms for them, the Christian seasons in honor of our Lord, the minor commemorations of the apostles, were subjected to the utmost scorn.

"In a word, Puritanism robbed religion of all that was high and noble and tender and graceful and winning and affectionate and reverent, and threw over her a dark, gloomy, and repulsive vestment; deprived her votaries of all the high and thrilling associations which the feeling of membership in Christ's holy Catholic Church and the Communion of Saints has such power to bestow, and could see no Christianity before the days of Calvin. Rejecting the authority of Œcumenical Councils, she bowed down before the Swiss pastor, and, careless of orthodoxy on cardinal points, assured her votaries of salvation, if they felt they were among the elect and abused to the best of their ability the Church of Rome.

"Such were the principles which Charles saw pervading the length and breadth of the land over which God's providence had caused him to reign. Brought up in the true principles of the Church of England, and himself no mean theologian, he saw at once that if this heresy obtained the upper hand, the Church of England would soon cease to be a witness for the 'faith once delivered to the saints,' and forfeit her claim to be considered a branch of the Church catholic. Laud saw the same thing, and the crosier and the sceptre entered into a firm alliance." * The House of Commons had lately taken upon themselves the office of Theological Inquisitors, and they began their work by seizing upon Montague, one of the King's chaplains, and committing him to the custody of the Sergeant-at-Arms, and this, not for any offence against the Government, but because, some time before, he had written a volume against Popery, containing remarks which the Calvinists did not fancy. Of course, Charles was indignant, and Laud, together with the Bishops of Rochester and Oxford, addressed Buckingham in his behalf, alleging

* *Baines's Life of Laud,* page 51.

that some of Montague's opinions were the doctrines of the Church, and others abstruse and difficult theological points which had always been left open. And they proceed: "May it please your Grace further to consider, that the clergy submitted themselves in the time of Henry VIII.; the submission was so made, that if any difference, doctrinal or other, fell in the Church, the King and the Bishops were to be the judges of it in the National Synod or Convocation, the King first giving leave under his broad seal, to handle the points in difference. But the Church never submitted to any other judge, neither indeed can she, though she would." And they conclude by expressing their confidence in Montague, and their satisfaction that the King was about to refer the matter to church consideration.

The dissolution of the Parliament, August 12, saved Montague for the present, but Charles's second Parliament, which met February 2, 1626, renewed the attack.

Laud stood by his friend, and protected him, even when the King (thus early showing signs of his chief fault, — indecision) faltered before the storm. The Parliament was dissolved, and Montague made Bishop of Chichester, 1627. Well might Laud exclaim, in view of what had just transpired, "Methinks I see a cloud arising and threatening the Church of England. God of His mercy, dissipate it!"

CHAPTER EIGHTH.

Laud's Second Visitation of his Diocese — Changes at Court during his Absence — The Good Fortune of the Lord Keeper begins to fail him — The Bishop of St. David's rises higher in Royal Favor—Charles's Coronation — Laud in his Element — " God save the King " — The Second Parliament — Laud's Sermon on the Blessedness of Unity — A Specimen of his Style — Evidences of his Popularity with the King — Another unfortunate Measure — Removal to the See of Bath and Wells — The People exhorted to contribute to the Support of the King — Upholding the Honor of God and the Authority of the Church — Rebuking the King for coming too late to Public Worship.

IN the summer of 1625, after the adjournment of Parliament, Laud set out for Wales, on his second visitation of his diocese.

It appears very singular to American readers, to find English bishops thus dividing their time between secular and religious affairs, but so long as Church and

State are united, such will no doubt continue to be the case.

Laud returned to London in the winter of 1626, and was surprised to find that great changes had taken place at Court during his absence. It seems that the Duke of Buckingham had become offended with the Lord Keeper Williams, for some cause or other, and as he never forgave an enemy, he tried to do him all the harm he could. Not being able to deprive him of his appointments in the Church, he persuaded the King to take from him the Great Seal of England; and no sooner had Williams begun to go down in the scale of fortune, than the Bishop of St. David's found himself rising in the royal favor. At the earnest request of his old friend, Bishop Neile, he was appointed to attend his Majesty, as Clerk of the Closet, and from this time he became Charles's confidential adviser in all important matters relating to the Church.

Laud was distinguished with especial

favor on the occasion of the King's coronation, which took place on Candlemas-day, (Festival of the Purification of the Blessed Virgin,) February 2.

Williams, being Dean of Winchester, would have been entitled, by virtue of his office, to make arrangements for this splendid ceremonial, but as he was out of favor with Charles, his place was supplied by the Bishop of St. David's. Laud was now in his element, and nothing could have pleased him better than to be engaged in such preparations. At the time appointed, Charles I. entered the doors of Westminster Abbey, amid the shouts and acclamaions of the multitude, and there, before the altar of the Lord, he took the oath of office, while prayers were offered in his behalf. The sign of the cross was made upon his forehead with holy oil, while the consecrating bishop thus addressed him: —

"Stand and hold fast from henceforth, the place to which you have been heir by the succession of your forefathers, being now delivered to you by the authority of Almighty God, and by the hands of all us the Bishops and servants of God. And as you see the clergy to come nearer the altar than others, so remember that in place convenient you give them greater honor, that the Mediator of God and man may establish you in the kingly throne, to be the Mediator between the clergy and laity, that you may reign forever with Jesus Christ, the King of Kings, and Lord of Lords, who with the Father and Holy Ghost, liveth and reigneth forever. Amen."

"Let him obtain favor for the people," continued the sacred strain, "like Aaron in the tabernacle, Elisha in the waters, Zacharias in the temple; give him Peter's keys of discipline, and Paul's doctrine."

Then he swore to confirm to the people of England the laws and customs granted by his predecessors; and they placed the crown of St. Edward on his head, and the people shouted, "God save the King!" On the 6th of February,

1626, King Charles met his second Parliament, when Laud, by special appointment, preached before him. His text was from the 122d Psalm, verses 3, 4, and 5. "Jerusalem is builded as a city that is at unity in itself," etc.*

The design of the preacher was to set forth the blessedness of unity,—and with this view, he dwelt upon the glories of Jerusalem, as a type of the Christian Church and State combined. As a specimen of the Archbishop's style of sermonizing, we shall give a few closing sentences.

"The first lesson of this day's evening prayer is Exod. 18. There is the story of Jethro's counsel to Moses, for assistance

* Among various valuable works which the writer collected, in order to prepare himself thoroughly to understand the character of Archbishop Laud, was a volume of his sermons, published in London in 1829, which contains this discourse in full. Whatever we may think of its views in regard to the divine right of kings, and other kindred questions, no one can help admiring the sincerity of the preacher, and his familiarity with the Scriptures, which enabled him to gather illustrations from every part.

of inferior officers. This was not the beginning of that great and parliamentary council, which after continued successful in the state of the Jews. For that was set after by God himself [Numbers ii.] ; yet I make no great doubt, but that the ease, which Moses found by that council, made him apt to see what more he needed; and so far at least occasioned the settling of the Sanhedrim.

"I take the *omen* of the day, and the *service* of the *Church* to bless it. That our *David* may be happy in this, and all other *Sessions* of *Parliament*, as their *Moses* was in his *council* of the Elders. That the King and his people may now, and at all times, meet in love, consult in wisdom, manage their council with temper, entertain no private business to make the public suffer; and when their consultation is ended, part in the same love that should ever bring King and People together. And let us pray, that our *Jerusalem*, both *Church* and *State*, which did never but flourish when it was at unity in itself, may now and ever continue in that *unity*, and so be ever successful, both at home and abroad. That in this unity the *Tribes* of the Lord, even all the families and kindreds of his people, may come up to the Church, to pray, and praise, and give thanks unto Him. That no tribe or persons for any pretences (for they are no better) may absent themselves from the Church and testimony of the Lord. That the seats of judgment, ecclesiastical and civil of all sorts, may not only be set, but set firmly, to administer the justice of God, and the King, unto His people. That all men may reverence and obey the House of David, who itself upon God, is the foundation of all these blessings. That God would bless both David and this people. That so the people may have cause to give thanks to God for David; and that David may have cause to take joy in the love and loyalty of his people; and bless God for both. Till from this *Jerusa-*

lem, and this *temple*, and these *thrones*, He and we all may ascend into that glorious state which is in heaven. And this Christ for His infinite mercy's sake, grant unto us: To whom," etc.

The blessedness of unity was a most appropriate subject, indeed, for such a stormy, unsettled time, but it required more than an able sermon to quiet the voice of civil discord. A great conflict had began, and while Laud was recommending peace, the opposite party, who regarded him with especial dislike, made ready for battle. He, however, had great influence with the King, which soon became manifest in a royal proclamation, forbidding any one from setting forth new-fangled religious opinions. This was another great mistake, which only served to arouse popular indignation. Departures from "the faith once delivered to the saints," are greatly to be deplored, but no enactments of law can make people orthodox in their opinions, and oblige them all to think alike.

When Laud had been Bishop of St. David's for five years, he was removed to the See of Bath and Wells, which had become vacant by the death of Dr. Lake. And here again we must express our regret that he did not, at this stage of his life, withdraw from political affairs, and devote himself exclusively to the Church. But Charles had begun to look to him for advice and counsel, and perhaps his own tastes led him to prefer the course which custom had rendered so familiar.

One of his first acts, after his change of bishoprics, was to draw up by order of Buckingham, instructions for the bishops and archbishops, for circulation through the kingdom, exhorting the people to contribute to the support of the monarch, who had been plunged into war by his Parliament, and then left by them without money. The conclusion is very beautiful and worthy of being recorded.

"The three great and useful judgments which He darts down upon disobedient and unthankful people, are pestilence, famine, and sword. The pestilence did never more rage in this kingdom than of late, and God was graciously pleased in mercy to hear the prayer which was made unto Him, and the ceasing of that judgment was little less than a miracle. The famine threatened us this present year, and it must have followed, had God rained down His anger a little later upon the fruits of the earth; but upon our prayers He stayed that judgment, and sent us a blessed season, and most beautiful harvest. The sword is the thing which we are now to look to, and you must call the people to their prayers again, against that enemy, that God will be pleased to send the like deliverance from this judgment also; that in the same mercy He will vouchsafe to strengthen the hands of His people: that He will sharpen their sword, but dull and turn the edge of that which is in our enemies' hands, that so, while some fight, others may pray for this blessing."

"In everything, by prayer, let your requests be made known unto God," saith the Apostle. Laud thoroughly believed this: prayer pervades this paper. So, too, his private devotions, under the head "Bellum," illustrate this feature of his religious character. The prayers are mostly, as will be seen, compiled from Holy Scripture, for Laud was no stranger to the language of the sacred volume.

"O my God, though mighty nations gather together on heaps, yet let them be broken in pieces; though they take counsel together, bring it to nought. For they pronounce a decree, yet it shall not stand, if Thou, O God, be with us. Be with us, therefore, O God, for Jesus Christ His sake. Amen.

"O make the wars to cease in all the world, break the bow, and knap the spear in sunder, and burn the chariot in the fire: that men may be still, and know that Thou art God: that Thou wilt be exalted among the heathen, and in the earth. Amen.

"Hast Thou forgotten us, O God? and wilt not Thou, O God, go forth with our hosts? O help us against the enemy: for vain is the help of man. O Lord, help us. Amen. O Lord, bless the King: all his commanders under him; and all his soldiers. Cover all their heads, his especially, in the day of battle. Teach all their hands to war, and their fingers to fight. And bless all the guides and conductors of his armies under him, with wisdom and courage, and faithfulness, and watchfulness, and diligence, and whatsoever else may lead on to good success. And set a happy end, we humbly beseech Thee, to all these bloody distractions, and restore peace, and preserve religion in integrity among us, even for Jesus Christ His sake. Amen."

His next step shall be given in his own words, and we shall see him upholding the honor of Almighty God, the authority of the Church, and the reverence due to consecrated houses of prayer, even before kings. Much as he loved Charles, he loved reverence more, and shrunk not when his duty called him, from rebuking one whose office and person he so deeply venerated.

"It was Friday, — November 14th, or thereabouts, — taking occasion, from the abrupt both beginning and ending of public prayer on the 5th of November, I desired his Majesty, King Charles, that he would please to be present at prayers, as well as sermon every Sunday; and that at whatsoever part of the prayers he came,* the priest then officiating might proceed to the end of the prayers. The most religious King not only assented to this request, but also gave me thanks. This had not before been done from the beginning of King James' reign to this day. Now, thanks be to God, it obtaineth."

* The custom was that when the King entered, prayers stopped, and preaching began.

CHAPTER NINTH.

A Dangerous Policy — Laud becomes involved in serious Difficulties — Others were found to advocate the same Dangerous Principles — The Third Parliament — A Sermon which different Parties heard with different Feelings — The Commons pass Sentence on Dr. Manwaring — A great Stretch of Power — The Offender is pardoned and patronized by the King — The Commons proceed to censure Buckingham and Laud — Charles remonstrates in vain — Laud's friendly Correspondence with some Foreign Protestants — Become Bishop of London — The Charge of his being a Romanizer shown to be groundless.

WE mentioned in the last chapter, that Laud had prepared a circular letter to be scattered throughout the kingdom, exhorting the people to contribute money to relieve the King from the serious embarrassments which war and other causes had brought upon him. The policy which dictated such instructions was by no means new, but it was certainly a very dangerous one, and if persisted in, it would have given the death-blow to a free constitution. Although Laud merely acted in this matter by direction of the King, it was most unfortunate that he allowed himself to be mixed up with it at all, — both for his own sake, and for the peace and welfare of the country. He was not left alone, however, for other zealous churchmen were found to advocate the same dangerous measures. Prominent among these were two clergymen, — Sibthorpe and Manwaring by name. They both preached boldly in defence of the arbitrary levy which had been proposed, and much difficulty was occasioned by their imprudent discourses.

Charles' third Parliament was opened by a sermon from Bishop Laud on the excellence of unity, from Ephesians iv. 3: "*Endeavoring to keep the unity of the spirit in the bond of peace.*" *

It should be borne in mind, that through

* This discourse will be found in *Archbishop Laud's Sermons,* (Rivingtons, London, 1829,) p. 173.

the ill-advised counsels of the Duke of Buckingham, England was involved in an unpopular war with France, and the enemies of the government were therefore not much inclined to listen patiently to a sermon coming from one for whom they cherished no friendly feelings. We can imagine the smile of derision which played over the countenances of some determined Puritans, and the looks of disapprobation which would be exchanged by others, during its delivery. The feelings of their hearts were soon plainly expressed in acts. The Commons resumed the exercise of their inquisitorial power, by drawing up a declaration against Dr. Manwaring for the discourses which he had ventured to deliver; and they finally sentenced him to imprisonment during the pleasure of the House, adding that he should pay a thousand pounds to the King, make humble acknowledgment of his offence, be suspended for three years from the ministry, forbidden ever to preach at Court again, and that his offensive books should be called in by proclamation, and publicly burned.

This was certainly a great stretch of power in those who were complaining so bitterly that their own privileges were interfered with; and we have no more right to overlook their unconstitutional proceedings, than we have to excuse the King and his adherents for their high-handed measures. Even if Dr. Manwaring's sermons were as dangerous as represented, still some regard to law should have been had, in the efforts which were made to bring him to punishment. But although the Commons thus expressed their feelings towards the offenders, Charles did not wait long before he showed how little he sympathized with them; for the session was hardly ended before he pardoned Manwaring, and promoted him to the Bishopric of St. David's.

But the work of opposition was only begun. From Manwaring, the House of Commons next proceeded to censure the conduct of Buckingham, whose name they had never before ventured to mention. Laud came in for his share of their indignation, and indeed nothing less could have been expected, considering how thoroughly he was identified with the King and his prime-minister, in their several unpopular measures. In vain did Charles send a message to the Commons, reminding them that the session was nearly ended, and it was too late to introduce any new business. "It was foreseen that a great tempest was ready to burst on the Duke; and in order to divert it, the King thought proper, upon a joint application of the Lords and Commons, to endeavor giving them satisfaction with regard to the petition of right. He came, therefore, to the House of Peers, and pronouncing the usual form of words, 'Let it be law, as is desired,' gave full sanction and authority to the petition. The acclamations with which the house resounded, and the universal joy diffused over the nation, showed how much this petition had been the object of all men's vows and expectations.

"It may be affirmed without any exaggeration, that the King's assent to the petition of right produced such a change in the government as was almost equivalent to a revolution, and by circumscribing, in so many articles, the royal prerogative, gave additional security to the liberties of the subject. Yet were the Commons far from being satisfied with this important concession. Their ill-humor had been so much irritated by the King's frequent evasions and delays, that it could not be presently appeased by an assent which he allowed to be so reluctantly extorted from him. Perhaps, too, the popular leaders, implacable and artful, saw the opportunity favorable; and, turning against the King those very weapons with which he had furnished them, resolved to pursue the victory.

"The bill, however, for five subsidies, which had been formerly voted, immediately passed the House; because the granting of that supply was, in a manner, tacitly contracted for, upon the royal assent to the petition; and had faith been here violated, no further confidence could have subsisted between King and Parliament. Having made this concession, the Commons continued to carry their scrutiny into every part of government. In some particulars their industry was laudable; in some it may be liable to censure."*

And here we pause in the regular course of the narrative, to speak of something which belongs to this period of Laud's life, and which has been generally overlooked. We refer to his friendly relations and correspondence with some of the foreign Protestants, not belonging to his own communion, whom he is so often represented to have regarded with feelings not only hostile, but actually malignant. From his own letters, written with no view to their ever being made public, we are enabled to gain an insight into his mind and heart, and thus to form a correct judgment of the man.

* Hume's England, vol. v. pages 44–5.

On the 15th of July, 1628, he was translated to the Bishopric of London; and while occupying this position, he thus addresses Gerard John Vossius, a German scholar of rare attainments, and a Professor of Rhetoric, Chronology, and History, but who by no means agreed with him in all his views of Church government and polity:—

"Your letters, always most grateful to me, arrived safely by the hands of Lord Stewart, who, together with the Rt. Hon. Lord Carleton, has very lately waited upon me. He delivered to me, together with your letters, your volume of Theses,—a truly wonderful monument of your ability. You call it imperfect, and promise that, by and by, your portfolio will bring it forth in an enlarged and better shape. If so, I rejoice for the Church's sake, and for your own; the one will be thereby profited, and the other honored. And I the more rejoice, because I hear that some of your admirers at Oxford have determined to print, and have actually begun to print your Theses, in an imperfect state. I have done my best to prevent anything of yours seeing the light in such a condition, and hope I have succeeded. I have written that you are about to publish them complete.

"I applaud you for what you propose to do respecting Baronius, and especially because you have resolved not to criticise his minutiæ. Assuredly, in a work so diffuse as his, it would take too much time to hunt after his smaller faults, and would weary the skilful and eager reader. What is of most consequence is, to show, with brevity, where Rome has departed furthest from the primitive Church, and to prove one's allegations demonstratively,—each of which points I have always flattered myself you could easily accomplish. In due time, therefore, I shall expect your commentaries on Baronius in the Latin tongue, and doubt not I shall find you there, as on other occasions, the vindicator of our times against supercilious ignorance.

"My misfortune was a serious one, and still clings to me, though I can crawl a little with the aid of a crutch. I no longer suffer pain in the injured part, only from weakness. This will be my daily guest till the year rolls round. If then it pleases to go away, my recovered agility will be like a return after absence to one's home; if not, I shall make it my aim to have an upright mind even in a halting body, and bow to circumstances.

"I have done all I could for your business, under the hindrances which have overtaken me; and I will still labor for you, to the utmost of my love and strength. I beg to commend the health of my soul, as well as my body, to your prayers; yours are never forgotten by me. One thing truly grieves me, that entangled as I am in business, I am almost an exile from my books, — the only things under God which I idolize. I am anxious you should know this, lest hereafter you think me unworthy the name of *student*. May you long fare well, is the prayer of your most devoted friend,

"WILLIAM LONDON."

The charge commonly made against Laud, and the one most readily believed, was this, — that he was a secret, intriguing Romanizer. Let the letter just quoted be read over again, and see how little reason can be found for such a grave accusation, in his most confidential correspondence. "Cardinal Baronius was Rome's favorite *thesaurus* for appeals to history, in the days when it was her fancy and fashion to appeal to history, rather than to development, for the maintenance of her cause. Baronius was her chief dependence against the embattled host that had risen up in the shape of Magdeburg centuriators, who, with wondrous toil and no inferior ability, had turned the testimony of century upon century (hence their name) against her strongest positions. Baronius, accordingly, was the Goliath ecclesiastic, who, as Rome fain would have it, had given heresy to the fowls of the air and the beasts of the field. And yet, this gigantic champion of Popery was the identical one whom Laud was conspiring with his friend to topple down; while his right-hand man, in such a formidable undertaking, was a Protestant of Calvinistic Holland!

"If Laud were a Papist, he must have been one so eminently disloyal, as to have contrived mischiefs, not to be matched unless by the benefits accruing from the reckless fealty of Loyola and his Jesuits. And they who can believe in such a paradoxical possibility, are beyond the range of argument. They are wrapped up in prejudices tougher than the seven bulls' hides of ancient shields; and an arrow driven from a catapult could hardly reach their seat of sensibility. We may, therefore, legitimately despair of them.

"This studied opposition to Romanism is, no doubt, the most important of the larger features of Laud's letters; but a smaller one is quite .as prevalent, namely, his continual allusions to his need of a friend's intercessions, and his requests, always earnest and frequently touching, for a remembrance at the throne of grace. Had such a feature been found in the letters of a Puritan, it would have been considered as evidence of fervent personal piety. Must we believe, (let our readers never forget, that this importunity of Laud's was not meant, like some old diaries we wot of, for the public eye,) *must* we believe, that in him this was the snivelling of hypocrisy, and 'a token of perdition?'

"Here we had intended that the comments on this letter should terminate; but there is something which has struck us as very impressive, in the *manner* in which Laud alludes to Baronius, beyond the *fact* of his allusion to him; and so we hope our readers will pardon a few words more. This letter proves that Laud knew not only *where* to assail Romanism most effectively, but *how* also to conduct the onset with most judgment and skill. It proves that he possessed in a marked degree, a faculty whose name tells a wrong tale about its prevalence, — we mean what is usually styled 'common sense.' This is a sense which learned men are apt to be devoid of. A very learned man, particularly, is too much inclined, in the management of controversies, to act like a lawyer, overflowing with material, who wastes more strength than is necessary on subordinate considerations.

"We see the same sterling common sense in Laud, in the manner in which he would have the erudite Vossius, the living library, the man of adamantine memory, conduct a warfare with the Romish historical corypheus. 'Strike,' he bids him, 'his salient points. Be brief. Show where Rome has deserted primitive antiquity, most glaringly. Make your conclusions demonstrative.' What peerless counsel! And had Vossius seized upon it, with the temper and the sagacity of its giver, his prodigious acquirements might have enabled him to be to the Babylon of Italy, what Darius was to the Babylon of Chaldea, some twenty-one centuries before. 'And Babylon, the glory of kingdoms, the beauty of the Chaldees' excellency, shall be as when God overthrew Sodom and Gomorrah.' (Isa. xiii. 19.) The spirit of such a prophecy might have been verified by ecclesiastical royalties of later date, had the advice of William Laud been heeded with aught of the solicitude and earnestness with which it was commended, reiterated, and pressed. And yet this same William Laud, it is fancied, was the secret friend and patron, nay, servile deputy, of the supremacy he was toiling to undermine! Oh, tell it not in Gath," &c.*

* *Church Review,* vol. vi. [1854,] page 543. This able article is from the pen of Dr. T. W. Coit.

CHAPTER TENTH.

Murder of the Duke of Buckingham — One sincere Mourner — Laud suspects the Puritans unjustly — His warm Reception at Court — More active than ever — Parliament spends Time to little Purpose — The King makes Concessions which avail Nothing — The Session abruptly closed — "Laud, look to thyself" — His Anxiety about the Church and State — Fresh Accession of Honors — Birth of the Prince of Wales — His Baptism — The Puritans refuse to share in the public Rejoicings — Laud's Prayer on the Birth of the Prince.

FROM the spirit of bitterness which the House of Commons had displayed towards the Duke of Buckingham, it required no great foresight to predict that when Parliament opened again, they would renew their assault upon him. But the assassin's knife saved him from their fury. One Felton, a man of ardent, but melancholy temper, who had served under the Duke as a lieutenant, and who had been refused a higher appointment which he desired, was the author of this crime.

Although the nation shed few tears on the death of the royal favorite, Laud wept for him with unaffected sorrow. "I will say no more," he writes to Vossius, "lest my heart should break, and my spirit take to flight. The man is dead to whom we both owe so much." And again, "I return to the unutterable sorrow which overwhelms me, for the slaughter of the illustrious Duke, ever to be deplored. I doubt not that he has reached heaven. We remain dwellers upon earth, which Astrea has abandoned. Consider well your own loss; mine is infinite."

That all this was not mere words is evident from the fact that Laud's distress upon this melancholy occasion threw him into a severe illness. Moreover, the language of his private devotions forbids the idea of any deceit or sham.

"O merciful God, Thy judgments are often secret, always just. At this time they were temporarily heavy upon the poor Duke of Buckingham, upon me, upon all that had the honor to be near him. Lord, Thou hast, I doubt not, given him rest, and light, and blessedness in Thee: give also, I beseech Thee, comfort to his lady; bless his children; uphold his friends; forget not his servants. Lay open the bottom of all that irreligious and graceless plot that spilt his blood. Bless and preserve the King from danger and from insecurity in these dangerous times. And for myself, Lord, though the sorrows of my heart are enlarged in that Thou gavest this most honorable friend into my bosom, and hast taken him again from me, yet, blessed be Thy Name, O Lord, Thou hast given me patience. I shall now see him no more till we meet at the resurrection. Oh make that joyful to us, and to all Thy faithful servants, even for Jesus Christ His sake. Amen."

Laud was firmly persuaded that the murder of Buckingham had been the work of the fierce and determined party who were opposed to the government, and hence his antipathy to Puritan principles became more deep and settled than before. In this, however, he undoubtedly did them injustice; and Felton, who died in penitence for his crime, had been urged on to its commission by his own ungoverned passions.

On the 9th of September, Laud attended the Court for the first time after the assassination of the Duke, and was received by the King with many marks of favor. Indeed, he now became the chief adviser in Church and State, — a dangerous office, and one which brought him to the block!

As additional honors were conferred upon him, he showed himself more active than ever in the performance of what he considered his duty. He began his career as Bishop of London by correcting some abuses which had grown up in the University of Oxford, in connection with the annual election of Proctors; and afterwards perceiving that the King's recent injunctions had been imperfectly observed, he advised His Majesty to order a reprint of the Thirty-nine Articles, with a Declaration prefixed, for the purpose of guarding them from misconstruction. This plan was accordingly adopted; and although the instrument contained no new principles, and threatened no arbitrary punishment, it was received by the unquiet spirits of the time with the greatest exasperation.

The Parliament which met on the 20th of January, 1629, instead of attending to matters of real moment, was occupied in theological discussions, equally wearisome and unimportant.

Laud knew full well how thoroughly he was hated by many of the members; and his heart was constantly lifted up in prayer, as his only relief from the heated atmosphere of controversy, and the ceaseless strife of tongues. His private devotions are full of supplications of this sort:—

"O Lord, I beseech Thee forgive mine

enemies all their sins against Thee, and give me that measure of Thy grace, that for their hatred I may love them, for their cursing I may bless them, for their injury I may do them good, and for their persecution I may pray for them. Lord, I pray for them; forgive them, for they know not what they do. Amen."

"God of peace and charity, give to all my enemies peace and charity, forgive all their sins, and deliver me from their snares, through Jesus Christ our Lord. Amen."

"O Lord, consider mine enemies, how many they are, and they bear a tyrannous hate against me. Lord, deliver me from them. Amen."

"Be merciful unto me, O God, for mine enemies would swallow me up, and many they are which fight against me, O Thou Most Highest! They gather together and keep themselves close, they mark my steps, because they lay wait for my soul. But when I was afraid, I trusted in Thee; and when I cry, then shall mine enemies turn back. This Thou wilt make me know, when Thou art with me; be with me, therefore, O Lord, and let me see deliverance. Amen."

"O Lord, let not them that are mine enemies triumph over me, neither let them wink with their eyes that hate me either without a cause or for Thy cause. Amen."

"O Lord God, in Thee have I put my trust; save me from all them that persecute me, and deliver me, lest they devour my soul like a lion and tear it in pieces while there is none to help. Lift up Thyself, O God, because of the indignation of mine enemies; arise up for me in the judgment which Thou hast commanded, that my help may still be from Thee, O God, who preservest them that are true of heart. Amen."

"Have mercy upon me, O God, consider the trouble which I suffer of them that hate me, O Thou that liftest me up from the gates of death. Amen."

"Hear my voice, O God, in my

prayer; preserve my life from fear of the enemy; hide me from the conspiracy of the wicked, and from the rage of the workers of iniquity. They have whet their tongues like a sword, and shoot out their arrows, even bitter words; Lord, deliver me from them. Amen."

Charles had been disposed of late to humor the caprices of the Commons so far as he could with any show of consistency, but all to no purpose. At last his patience was worn out, and on the 2d of March he sent a message to the Houses, *commanding* their adjournment. The speaker was about to leave the chair, in obedience to this order, when he was forcibly detained in it until three resolutions were passed: the *first* against innovations in religion; the *second* against those who should advise the levying of taxes without the consent of Parliament; and the *third* against those who should yield a voluntary submission to the exaction. All such persons were denounced as enemies of the country;

and then, in the midst of the utmost confusion, the House adjourned.

Public indignation was not only aroused against Charles, but Laud, who was supposed to be his counsellor in all things, was roundly abused. One Sunday, not long after the adjournment of Parliament, two papers were found on the ground, the one directed against the Lord Treasurer, Weston, and the other to this effect,—"Laud, look to thyself. Be assured thy life is sought. As thou art the fountain of all wickedness, repent thee of thy monstrous sins, before thou be taken out of the world. And assure thyself, that neither God nor the world can endure such a vile counsellor or whisperer to live."

The only notice which he took of this furious attack was this brief record in his diary: "Lord, I am a grievous sinner, but I beseech Thee deliver my soul from them that hate me without a cause."

The extreme anxiety which he felt in regard to the perilous condition of Church and State, is seen in his letters to Vossius.

In January, 1629, he says: "So may God love me, I know not what can be done, especially by myself, for the Church, in these festering times." Again, in July, 1629, "Although I am unequal to the task of stilling the tempests by which the Church is tossed, yet you well know that, with the blessing of God, I will not be wanting to her cause, or my own duty. In the mean time, it is evident to all how deeply the State must be perilled, while the Church is drifting."

In the midst of all his cares, however, a fresh accession of honors now awaited him. On the 10th of April, 1630, the office of Chancellor of the University of Oxford became vacant by the sudden death of William, Earl of Pembroke. On the 12th, the Bishop of London was chosen to supply his place. In spite of some hasty opposition which was offered by the Calvinistic party, with the aid of the four colleges belonging to the Visitation of Dr. Williams, as Bishop of Lincoln, his election was carried with little difficulty. This unsolicited distinction must, doubtless, have been signally gratifying. The Bishop, nevertheless, was anxious to decline the burdensome and invidious honor. But his objections were overruled by His Majesty, who gladly and graciously approved of the appointment. On the 28th of April he was solemnly invested with the office. And the rest of his life shows how solicitous he was to justify the choice of the University, by his sleepless care for its prosperity, and by additional splendor of munificence in the encouragement of letters.

In the course of another month, he received a farther mark of the royal favor and regard. On the 29th of May the Queen was safely delivered of a Prince, afterwards Charles the Second; and Laud "had the happiness to see him before he was full one hour old." On the 27th of June the royal infant was baptized by the

Bishop, as Dean of the Chapel Royal,— the Archbishop, to whom the performance of the rite more properly belonged, being absent, either from infirmity or from a feeling of alienation towards the Court.

The event was hailed with joy by all but the Puritanical party. Their hopes and affections were fixed on the family of the Queen of Bohemia, sister to their king. Her children, they said, were brought up in the Reformed religion. But how could any man know what would be the religion of the king's children, seeing they were nurtured by a mother so devoted to the Church of Rome? And hence, while the rest of the kingdom was ringing with festivity, the Calvinists wore an aspect of almost funereal sorrow. Heylin tells us that he was at a town in Gloucestershire when the intelligence arrived, and that, in honor of it, the bells rang, and the bonfires blazed, and good cheer was distributed. But, all this time, "from the house of the Presbyterians there came neither man, nor child, nor wood, nor victuals; their doors being shut close all the evening, as in a time of general mourning and disconsolation."

We close our chapter with the prayer called forth by the birth of the Prince of Wales, which Laud so devoutly offered up to the King of Kings, —

"Oh, most merciful God and gracious Father, Thou hast given us the joy of our hearts, the contentment of our souls for this life, in blessing our dear and dread sovereign and his virtuous royal queen with a hopeful son, and us with a prince, in Thy just time and his to rule over us. We give Thy glorious Name most humble and hearty thanks for this. Lord, make us so thankful, so obedient to Thee for this great mercy, that Thy goodness may delight to increase it to us. Increase it, good Lord, to more children, the prop one of another against single hope; increase it to more sons, the great strength of his Majesty and his throne; increase it in the joy of his royal parents, and all true-hearted subjects; increase it by his Christian and happy education both in faith and goodness, that this kingdom and people may be happy in the long life and prosperity of our most gracious sovereign and his royal consort. And when fulness of days must gather them, Lord, double his graces, and make them apparent in this his heir, and his heirs after him for all generations to come, even for Jesus Christ His sake, our Lord and only Saviour. Amen."

CHAPTER ELEVENTH.

Restoring St. Paul's Cathedral to its former Glory — A noble Example, which provokes Puritan Hostility — Charles's first Visit to Scotland — Fears which were soon realized — The "Southern Church" set up — The Scottish Bishops invested with Civil Offices — A Dream of Complacency and Satisfaction — Laud succeeds to the Primacy — The Conflict between two Great Principles drawing on — The Head of two Famous Universities — No Pride or Exultation manifested — Letter to Strafford — Laud's Courage equal to his Greatness — The Jesuits show their Hand — Offer of a Cardinal's Hat — An Injury done whether accepted or refused — The Tempter departs.

WHEN Laud received his appointment as Bishop of London, it distressed him to see the condition of St. Paul's Cathedral, which was then in a state of ruinous dilapidation. With his usual energy, he immediately formed plans for its restoration, and set the example of liberality himself, by contributing about five hundred dollars a year (£100) for this purpose. He also inspired others with his own enthusiasm, and in the course of eight or nine years more than £100,000 were raised towards wiping out this national reproach.

The Puritans looked on with suspicion, and spoke in no measured terms against the folly of repairing and beautifying a *rotten relique,* as they profanely called the temple of the Lord. Besides this, Laud did many noble things for the University of Oxford, and especially for his own college, which he adorned with an additional quadrangle, and an elegant gallery.

In 1633, King Charles made his first visit to Scotland. He reached Edinburgh on the 10th of June, and on the 18th of the same month his coronation took place, at Holyrood House, with unusual pomp and magnificence.

The people gave him a warm welcome, although fears were entertained that his Majesty would attempt to carry out his father's plans, and set up among them what they called the *Southern Church.* These apprehensions were not diminished when they saw Laud performing divine service in the royal chapel according to the rites of the English Prayer-Book. His sermon was rather more prudent than usual, and it was listened to with apparent satisfaction, although he recommended in the strongest terms the adoption of the same ritual throughout the King's dominions.

Charles was encouraged by the favorable appearance of affairs to push forward his favorite measure; and he even ventured to establish Edinburgh as a new Bishopric, — a step which was regarded as a national grievance. He also, most unwisely, invested the Scottish bishops with the highest civil offices of the kingdom, hoping, in this way, to add to their influence among the people. So far was this from being the case, it excited the envy and indignation of the nobility, and surrounded the bishops themselves with enemies and spies.

The King and his spiritual adviser must indeed have been laboring under a species of insanity, to propose measures so fatal to the prosperity of the Church; and they actually returned to London in a dream of complacency and satisfaction, fondly believing that a great triumph had been achieved for the cause of true religion.

The death of Archbishop Abbot now enabled Charles to advance the Bishop of London to the Primacy; and the clothier's son has at length reached a dignity which must have gratified his worldly ambition, and, at the same time, opened to him a field of unbounded usefulness. As Archbishop of Canterbury, Primate of all England, and a member of the Privy Council, Laud stood in importance next to the throne. Yet the years of his greatness were to be few; and even these, clouded as they were with sorrow, were to be the precursors of a fearful fall. The storm which for a long while had been slowly gathering was now rapidly darkening the horizon, and as men gazed upon it "their hearts failed them for fear, and for looking after those things which were coming on the earth." Deep was calling unto deep, and on every side were the signs of the gathering strife. The least discerning could perceive that the conflict between the two great principles was drawing on, and that soon it would be brought to open issue. The two parties which divided the kingdom were assuming definite forms; and the names of Cavalier and Roundhead began to have a meaning and significance which they will never lose as long as history lasts.

The elevation of Laud to the Primacy occasioned no surprise; as the King and himself were of the same mind in Church matters, and no one could possibly have been found more anxious to carry out the wishes of his Majesty. Honors now came thick and fast. He was elected Chancellor of the University of Oxford, and soon afterwards the same office in the University of Dublin was conferred upon him.

It was not without fear and trembling that he accepted of these various honorable appointments; and his private devotions show that humiliation and self-communion and fasting and prayer were not forgotten at a time when there was so much to dazzle and distract his mind. His letter to Strafford manifests no pride nor exultation, —

"I heartily thank your lordship," he writes, "for all your love, and for the joy you are pleased both to conceive and express for my translation to Canterbury; for I conceive all your expressions to me are very hearty, and such as I have hitherto found them. And now, since I am there, I must desire your lordship not to expect more at my hands than I shall be able to perform, either in Church or State; and this suit of mine hath a good deal of reason in it, for you write that ordinary things are far beneath that which you cannot choose but promise yourself of me in both respects. But, my lord, to speak freely, you may easily promise more in either kind than I can perform; for, as for the

Church, it is so bound up in the forms of the common law, that it is not possible for me or for any man to do that good which he would, or is bound to do. For your lordship sees — no man clearer — that they which have gotten so much power in and over the Church, will not let go their hold; they have indeed fangs with a witness, whatsoever I was once said in passion to have. And for the State, my lord, indeed I am for thorough; but I see that both thick and thin stays somebody where I conceive it should not, and it is impossible for me to go through alone. Besides, I doubt I shall never be able to hold my health there one year; for, besides all the jolting which I had over the stones, between London House and Whitehall, which was almost daily, I shall now have no exercise, but slide over in a barge to the Court and Star Chamber. And in truth, my lord, I speak seriously; I have had a heaviness hang upon me ever since I was nominated to this place, and I can give myself no account of it, unless it proceed from an apprehension that there is more expected from me than the craziness of these times will give me leave to do."

That Laud's courage was equal to his greatness is also evident from the tone of his correspondence: — "I am resolved," he writes on another occasion, "to go steadily forward in the way you have seen me go. I hope God will give me constancy and patience, and I heartily desire that you will commend me to His protection by your prayers. Thus fortified, I will go forward whithersoever He shall lead me."

And his devotions record the fervor with which he himself sought for strength at the Throne of Grace: —

"O God, the Pastor and Guide of all the faithful, mercifully regard me Thy servant, who Thou hast willed should preside over the Church of Canterbury; grant me, I most humbly beseech Thee, to profit both by word and example those over whom I am set, that, together with the flock intrusted to me, I may attain to everlasting life, through Jesus Christ our Lord. Amen.

"O my God, most merciful Father, may Thy grace so work in me that I may be humble in refusing all great office, but prepared in undertaking, faithful in preserving, strenuous in following it out, vigilant in ruling Thy people, earnest in correcting them, ardent in loving them, patient in bearing with them, prudent in restraining them, that I may be between those over whom I am set and God when consulting for their good, and offer myself to Him, when angry, in faith, and for the merits of Jesus Christ our Saviour.

"O Lord, as the rain cometh down from heaven, and returns not thither, but waters the earth, and makes it bud and bring forth, that it may give seed to the sower and bread to him that eateth, so let Thy Word be that goeth out of my mouth; let it not return to me void, but accomplish that which Thou wilt, and prosper in the thing whereto Thou hast sent it, that the people committed to my charge may go out with joy, and be led forth in peace to Thy freshest waters of comfort, in Jesus Christ, our Lord. Amen.

"O Son of God, Thou which takest away the sins of the world, have mercy upon me in this heavy charge. Amen."

The Puritans had been so sure that Laud would succeed Abbot as Archbishop of Canterbury, that his elevation to that office occasioned no fresh outburst amongst them, and they determined quietly to abide their time. The emissaries of the Pope, on the other hand, were more than usually busy, and the Jesuits practised some of their most dangerous arts. The remains of Abbot were hardly laid in the grave before some persons, whose names are now unknown, called upon his intended successor, with the insidious offer of a Cardinal's hat. Laud thus speaks of it in his journal: —

"August 4th. That very morning, at Greenwich, there came one to me, seriously, and that avowed ability to perform it, and offered me to be a Cardinal. I went presently to the King, and acquainted him both with the thing and the person.

"August 17th. I had a serious offer made to me again to be a Cardinal. I was then from Court, but so soon as I came thither, (which was Wednesday, August 21,) I acquainted his Majesty with it. But my answer again was, that *somewhat dwelt within me which would not suffer that till Rome were other than it is.*"

This was a crafty plan, indeed, and one worthy of the disciples of Loyola. Whether Laud accepted or refused the offer from Rome, the purposes of its authors would be gained. If accepted, it would convert the Pope's formidable enemy into a firm friend, and if refused, it might help to ruin him, by creating a suspicion that he was in secret correspondence with Rome.

The tempter came twice, as we have seen, and after the second refusal he appeared no more.

CHAPTER TWELFTH.

The Chapel at Lambeth — A Visitation of the Province of Canterbury begun — Another unpleasant Difficulty with Bishop Williams — Laud endeavors to bring the Foreign Protestants into closer Conformity with the English Church — How shamefully some English Chaplains behaved when beyond the Seas — Nurseries of Disaffection — "A kind of God's Israel in Egypt" — Successful Efforts in Behalf of the Church in Ireland — Two noble Spirits who will pay dearly for their zealous Labors.

AS Primate of the English Church, Laud of course resided at Lambeth, which for so long a period had been the abode of the chief dignitary of the Church. Archbishop Abbot had been careful enough to keep the *palace* in good repair; and this was disfigured by no broken roofs or patched windows; but the *chapel* belonging to it had been so shamefully neglected that it had fallen into the most dreadful state of dilapidation and decay. The beautiful stained-glass windows, containing the leading incidents in our Saviour's life, and other sacred pictures, had all been battered and broken, and patched up in the rudest manner; and everything about the little chapel showed that it had suffered greatly from the sad effects of fanatical zeal and careless indifference.

Laud took peculiar pains in restoring it, as far as he was able, to its former condition; and strange to say, this very attempt to show honor to the Lord's house, was numbered at last among his heinous offences. But his attention was by no means confined to his own palace, or to the adornments of his private chapel. Early in 1634, he resolved to make a visitation of the whole province of Canterbury, and to correct the many irregularities and abuses which had so long disgraced the Church. Of course, he encountered much opposition in the accomplishment of this purpose, and the difficulty was increased from the fact that Bishop Williams set his face against it. So far as restoring the altar to its proper place, and other changes of the sort were concerned, the Bishop of Lincoln had no serious objection; indeed, the proper arrangement of the chancel was preserved in his own cathedral, and in several other churches of his diocese; but he had an old grudge against the Archbishop, and it was not his intention to yield to him if he could possibly avoid it.

When we behold a world lying in wickedness, needing the combined efforts of all the ministers of the Lord Jesus to bring it to a knowledge of the truth, alas, how painful to see brethren of the same household of faith thus estranged from one another, and by their bitter enmity doing incalculable injury to the cause of God!

Laud heard of some proceedings of the Bishop of Lincoln which appeared like a signal of hostility to his proposed reform, and he therefore determined to make that diocese the scene of his first visitation. Williams, as was natural enough, showing a disposition to rebel, the Archbishop deprived him of his jurisdiction until he had gone through the diocese and arranged everything according to his own notions of propriety. This unhappy encounter between the two high-toned prelates served to widen the breach between them; and as we shall discover in the sequel, the Bishop of Lincoln lived to enjoy the luxury of retribution.

Another arbitrary act charged upon Laud, was his attempt to force upon the foreign Protestants the Liturgy and discipline of the English Church. While he was Bishop of London, he had heard with extreme regret of the inexcusable irregularities which prevailed among the English factories and regiments in other countries. The chaplains stationed beyond the seas, either to escape from opposition, or to court popularity, had laid aside the Prayer-Book, and the peculiarities of the Church to which they belonged, and conducted public worship according to the customs of Presbyterian Geneva. In insisting that such abuses should be corrected he certainly acted wisely.

Another and more difficult question was now proposed to him by the Council, and this related to the French and Walloon churches in England. It was a settled maxim of the State that the nation was to follow the faith of the Prince. Nay, half a century later, English people so little understood toleration, that they drove James II. from the throne for his endeavors to bring it about. So that we cannot condemn Laud if his conduct with regard to these foreigners was different from the maxims of the nineteenth century. His dislike of the foreigners was shared by the Puritan Bishop Williams, who had formerly dissuaded King James from allowing a number of Bohemians to settle here, and Laud's argument before the Council (while he praised the piety of the State in allowing them a shelter when persecuted), was, that it never could be intended they were to exist for generations. The truth is, they were nurseries of disaffection, — seed-plots of sedition and false doctrine; and it seemed inconsistent to restrain English Puritanism and encourage the foreign. Laud could not understand the right or reason of so doing.

The religious tenets of the foreign bodies were of the strongest kind of Calvinism, — their political ones were closely allied to republicanism. The bad character they brought with them clung to them in the country of their adoption. They formed a rallying-point for the Puritans, who encouraged them with all sorts of flattery, by telling them the maintenance of the Gospel depended upon them, and that they were the destined instruments for ridding the Church of England of the tyranny of the bishops.

Politically too they were dangerous; and their religious assemblies exempted from the ecclesiastical law, might easily be made schools of treason. Laud himself says that he invaded no privileges, that he only interfered with them because they did not use their privileges and immunities with gratitude to His Majesty, the State, and the Church of England, as they ought to have done. He said at his trial:—

"1. That their living as they did and standing so strictly to their own discipline, wrought upon the party in England which were addicted to them, and made them more averse than otherwise they would have been to the present government of the Church of England.

"2. That by this means they lived in England as if they were a kind of God's Israel in Egypt, to the great dishonor of the Church of England, to which at first they fled for shelter against persecution. And in that time of their danger, the Church of England was in their esteem not only a true but a glorious Church. But by this favor which that Church received, it grew up and encroached upon us till it became a Church within a

Church, and a kind of State within a State. And this I ever held dangerous, how small beginning soever it had, and that upon two main reasons. The one because I find the wisdom of God against it. For He says plainly to His prime people, one law, (and especially for Divine worship,) shall be to him that is home born, and to the stranger that sojourns among you. [Exod. xii.] And the other, because I find the wisdom of the State against it. For this, Parliament in their remonstrance give the self-same reason against the Papists, which must hold good against all sects that labor to make strong and enlarge themselves. The words are these: 'Another State, moulded within this State, independent in government, contrary in interest and affection, secretly corrupting the ignorant or negligent professors of our religion, and closely uniting and combining themselves against such as are sound, in this posture waiting for an opportunity, &c.' And the words are as true of the one faction as of the other; and I ever pressed the argument against both, as I can prove by good witnesses, if need be. And I pray God this faction, too little feared and too much nourished among us, have not now found the opportunity waited for."

Many of the members of the foreign communions were the native subjects of the English king, and in those days when religious toleration was a doctrine which no party inculcated, it was plainly in accordance with the laws of the land, that they should be expected to obey.

In 1634, when Laud began to make inquiries concerning the French and Dutch congregations in England, they at once set up the claim of exemption from his jurisdiction, on account of letters-patent received in the days of Edward VI., and afterwards confirmed by acts of Council in the reigns of Elizabeth, King James, and his present Majesty. The Archbishop was, notwithstanding, inflexible. It was, of course, well known to him that letters-patent had been granted by Henry VIII. to John Alsaco and his congregation of strangers. But it was also known that these same congregations were utterly broken up in the time of Queen Mary, and that their privileges departed with them. He, likewise, recollected — though the congregations seem to have forgotten it — that the policy of Elizabeth, with reference to the foreign churches, was distinctly recorded in a letter of hers to the Lord Treasurer Pawlet, signed with her own hand, in the second year of her reign, in which she signifies her pleasure that the Church of Augustine Friars should be delivered to the Bishop of London, for the use of strangers resorting to the city; and that such ministers as he might approve should be appointed to those churches, but "so as no rite nor use be therein observed contrary or derogatory to her laws."

With this memorial of the "wisdom of those times" before him, the Archbishop persevered; and, after some contentious negotiation, it was ordained that those ministers and others of the French and Dutch congregations who were not native subjects of the King, should be allowed to use their own discipline as before; but that, nevertheless, the English Liturgy should be translated into French and Dutch, in order that the children of the foreigners should be brought up in the communion of the Church of England. It was further ordered, that in future none but strangers should be admitted as ministers in those congregations, and that the natives should be bound to make collections for the maintenance of their own ministry and the poor of their own church. This last injunction was added to pacify the apprehensions which had arisen lest these proceedings should so far have the effect of *naturalizing* the congregations as to entitle their poor to relief out of the parish rates."

Great credit is due to Laud for his successful exertions in behalf of the poor, oppressed Church in Ireland. We have not time to enlarge upon this, but can only say that through his influence with Charles the revenues of the Church, which had been unrighteously employed for other purposes, were restored to her, and many gross irregularities corrected. In this important work he found an able assistant in the Earl of Strafford, the Lord Deputy of Ireland; and the two kindred spirits labored together with the utmost harmony until, in 1634, a Convocation was held in Dublin, and the English Articles and Canons being adopted, the churches of England and Ireland were brought into a state of conformity with each other.

We shall meet the noble-hearted pair again in very different circumstances.

CHAPTER THIRTEENTH.

Laud's unpopular Manners make him many Enemies — His Metropolitan Visitation continued, with such Results as might have been expected — Some real Good which he accomplished — The famous William Prynne and his two Worthy Associates — Fining and Ear-cropping — The Barbarities of the Star-Chamber — Bishop Williams betrays the King's Secrets — He suffers well for his gossiping Disposition — Fresh Troubles in Scotland — A Memorable Sunday in Edinburgh — Divine Service celebrated under very disgraceful Circumstances — "A Pape, a Pape; pull him down!" — Laud's last Effort for the Scotch Church.

ARCHBISHOP Laud might have been a much more popular man than he was had he cultivated the graces of manner, and endeavored to make himself agreeable to those with whom he was brought in contact. But he seems to have paid little attention to the common courtesies of life, and being naturally of an irritable temper, and accustomed to speak out plainly all that he thought, he provoked the enmity of many who might otherwise have been his friends. Clarendon, who knew him well, and appreciated his good points, tells us that "he was a man of great courage and resolution, and being most assured within himself that he proposed no end in all his actions or designs than what was pious and just, (as sure no man had ever a heart more entire to the King, the Church, or the Country,) he never studied the best ways to those ends; he thought, it may be, that any art or industry that way would discredit, at least make the integrity of the end suspected, let the cause be what it will. He did court persons too little; nor cared to make his designs and purposes appear as candid as they were, by showing them in any other dress than their own natural beauty and roughness; and did not consider enough what men said, or were like to say of him."

This insight into his character will enable us to account for some of the difficulties which so unhappily beset his way.

We find him, in 1635, prosecuting the unpopular visitation begun in the previous year; and a great deal of talking and writing and disputing about the arrangement of altars and the proper mode of conducting the services was the result. The Archbishop was no doubt perfectly right in regard to most of these things; but it was a sad pity that he did not proceed in this work with less precipitation, and manifest greater patience and moderation.

He really accomplished very much in restoring the cathedrals to a fit condition for the becoming celebration of public worship; and his enlightened munificence in enriching the University of Oxford with literary treasures in the shape of ancient manuscripts, and in making provision for the proper cultivation of Hebrew and Arabic, and other languages, is beyond all praise.

But we have some other matters to mention, far less agreeable than these.

The more that the zealous Archbishop labored to promote the interests of the church which he loved so dearly, the more fierce was the spirit of opposition excited against him. Prynne, Burton, and Bastwick made themselves very conspicuous in this contest.

William Prynne was an Oxford scholar, afterwards admitted to the Bar, who from his boyhood had been infected with Puritan principles, and in course of time he became almost insane on religious subjects. He published some very severe things against amusements, and even employed his caustic pen in ridiculing the music of the cathedrals and the festivities of Christmas.

The Puritans were proud of one who could thus lash all parties that displeased them; and not only bishops and nobles, but the members of the royal family, felt the effect of his blows.

Prynne had two able supporters in John Bastwick and Henry Burton, — the first a physician, and the other a clergyman.

These infatuated zealots were brought before the High Court, called the Star Chamber,* where they were tried for their offences, and sentenced to receive a most severe and cruel punishment. Besides the payment of a large fine, their ears were cropped, and they were then cast into prison. The three champions of Puritanism endured this frightful punishment with astonishing heroism; and, as may readily be supposed, a thousand times more injury was done to the King and his cause by the barbarous sen-

* "A room in the House of Lords, so called from having its ceiling adorned with gilded stars, or, according to some, because it was originally the place of deposit of the Jewish starrs (starra) or covenants. The despotic tribunal, which sat here, was also called the star-chamber. It was under the direction of the chancellor, and had jurisdiction of forgery, perjury, riots, maintenance, fraud, libel, and conspiracy, and, in general, of every misdemeanor, especially those of public importance, for which the law had provided no sufficient punishment. It was this criminal jurisdiction (its civil having gone into disuse) that made it so powerful and odious an auxiliary of a despotic administration. Its process was summary, and often iniquitous, and the punishment which it inflicted often arbitrary and cruel. It became particularly violent in the reign of Charles I.; and it was abolished, with the no less hateful High Commission Court, by the long parliament in 1641. Its fall was an important step in the progress of English liberty." — *Encyclopædia Americana*, Vol. XI., page 565.

tence of the court than the writings and ravings of these crazy enthusiasts could ever have accomplished. Sympathy was excited in their behalf, and indignation was very freely expressed.

Archbishop Laud has generally received the largest share of censure for these absurd and cruel proceedings, although he does not really deserve it. Every member of the court except himself voted for the sentence; but he declined doing so, on the ground that the worst abuse of the offenders had been heaped upon himself, and he did not wish thus to seem to return evil for evil. He did not hesitate to express his opinion, however, very decidedly, as to the infamous libels which Prynne and his companions had so diligently circulated. We have no excuse to offer for the cruel proceedings of the Star Chamber, although it is but just to say, that these bloody reliques of an uncivilized age were rather the fault of the times than of the individuals.

In 1637 Bishop Williams was brought

into public notice again, and that, too, in a very disagreeable way. It seems that some time before, the King, having become alarmed at the dissatisfaction which was spreading among his subjects, sought a private interview with the Bishop, in which he asked his advice as to the best course to be pursued in order to win back the confidence of the Commons, knowing that Williams was a favorite with the Puritan faction, and had considerable influence with them. Williams suggested the propriety of secretly instructing the officers of government to show more favor to the Puritans, as their increasing numbers made it highly important that their good will should be secured.

Charles had already thought of this plan himself, and therefore he was the more ready to adopt it.

Bishop Williams had given good advice; and something might thus have been accomplished for healing the unhappy divisions in the kingdom but for a gossiping disposition which prevented him from keeping his own secrets. He was even so imprudent as to speak of his interview with Charles, at a dinner-table, in the presence of several persons, who spread the information around until it reached the ears of his Majesty. It was a grave offence for a Privy Councillor to reveal the secrets of the King, and Williams was arraigned and condemned to pay a heavy fine and be imprisoned in the Tower.

A search among his private papers brought to light some correspondence carried on with one Osbaldston, formerly master of Westminster School, and then a Prebendary of Westminster, in which disrespectful references were made to Archbishop Laud and others. This discovery led to another prosecution, and Williams and Osbaldston were both fined, — the latter being deprived of his preferments, and condemned to have his ears nailed to the pillory.

He lost his money and his position in the Church, but he saved his ears by flight;

while Williams remained in the Tower until November, 1640, when he was released by an order of the House of Lords, and restored to his place on the bench of Bishops. The King soon after received him into favor again, and by his direction the record of all proceedings against him was destroyed.

But there have been stirring times in Scotland, and we must beg our readers to accompany us thither once more.

Archbishop Laud had done his best to persuade the Scottish Bishops to adopt the English Prayer-book, but they preferred to show their independence by making some changes in it. Several years passed away before all parties were satisfied; but at last the Scotch Prayer-book was completed, and a royal proclamation was sent forth towards the close of 1636, directing it to be used on the following Easter. For some unimportant reasons this order was not carried into effect until the 23d of July, 1637,—by which time the Scotch people had become very much alarmed by reports which were diligently circulated, representing the Prayer-book as only another name for the Romish Missal, and as a fresh instrument of the King's arbitrary power. Pamphlets were published, inflaming the public mind; meetings were held, and no efforts were spared to excite the populace to desperate deeds.

The 23d of July was destined to be a memorable Sunday in Edinburgh. The Presbyterians, according to the preconcerted scheme, thronged the principal churches. Their plans had been all arranged beforehand by the preacher Henderson, Lord Balmerino, and Sir T. Hope; even the old women, who played such a conspicuous part, were ready drilled, and were encouraged to commence the uproar by the assurance that the men would take it, — and for this purpose some men were actually dressed in women's attire, and placed at their post. Archbishop Spotswood as Lord Chancellor, the Archbishop of Glasgow, several Bishops, Lords of the Council, and Magistrates of the city wended their way on that "stony Sabbath" — as the Scots called it — to St. Giles' Church. They were surrounded by all the insignia and paraphernalia of their office, that nothing might be wanting to shed a lustre of importance round the inauguration of a work the King was known to have so much at heart.

At nine in the morning the Dean began the service. And then, fearing neither God nor King, unawed by the sanctity of the place or sacredness of the occasion, the true fanatical, ignorant, irreverent Puritan spirit burst forth. Instead of falling on their knees and confessing their sins, they hooted, they shouted, they hissed, they stamped, they swore, they blasphemed, they gave vent to all sorts of filthy indecencies, and called it religion. The Dean went on, and then they raged still more furiously. Amid oaths, and curses, and ribald jests, they flung Bibles, stones, sticks, stools at his head; they advanced to the prayer-desk, and seized hold of him; but he escaped, leaving his surplice in their hands.

In vain Bishop Lindsay ascended the pulpit, and strove to recall the fanatic horde to a sense of decency and respect for the consecrated dwelling of the Almighty. They only howled the more, and made him the aim of their missiles. The Chancellor rose, but his voice was drowned immediately in a chorus of imprecations. As the chief civil authority, he straightway ordered the magistrates to clear the church. With great difficulty his orders were obeyed, the doors locked, and the service concluded; but the populace, not to be baulked of their unholy sport, battered the windows with stones, and raised the Puritan war-cry till they were hoarse, — "A Pape! — a Pape! — Pull him down!"

When the bishops left the church they found the streets crowded by a mob of ruffians clamoring for vengeance. They had already profaned the Lord's Day and desecrated a church, — the latter a special treat for Puritans; but if they could have killed a bishop their joy would have known no bounds. The life of the Bishop of Edinburgh was only saved by the servants of Lord Wemyss carrying the prelate by force into their master's house. Evening prayer was said with closed doors; but the godless crew again sought the Bishop's life on his return. Not even the presence of the popular Lord Roxburgh, in whose carriage he was, protected him. They assaulted the coach, and the swords of the soldiers alone saved him. And so ended this memorable Sunday, the greatest exhibition of profanity and wickedness perpetrated under the name of religion by any so-called religious party. The Puritans professed to be the only spiritually-minded people of their day. We have here a specimen of their right to what they claimed. They claimed to have a great veneration for the Sunday, yet they scrupled not to disgrace it by riots unparalleled in the annals of the Church, with the exception of those raised by the Arians in primitive times against the professors of the Orthodox faith.

Laud felt that unless the most decided measures were adopted all hope for the Scotch Church would be lost; and his letters on the subject are full of stirring eloquence. But we need not inform our readers that his efforts were in vain. Scotland rejected Episcopacy, and cast in her lot with Calvinism. She has reaped many bitter fruits thereof.

CHAPTER FOURTEENTH.

Laud turns his Attention to the Channel Islands — Saving the young Theologians the Trouble of going abroad to pick up False Doctrine — Chillingworth and his great Work — How his conscientious Godfather snatched him from the Toils of Romanism — The Suppression of Fanatical Publications — Curious Bible Notes, which Kings and Bishops did not relish — Two Inflammatory Papers — John Lilburn — Laud's Letter to the Helvetic Pastors — Protesting his Desire for Peace — Unites with Strafford and Hamilton in recommending a Parliament.

WHEN Archbishop Laud had finished the Visitation in England, — which had produced so much controversy and confusion, but which ultimately accomplished some good, — he turned his attention to the Channel Islands. The inhabitants had been accustomed to send their young men who were looking forward to the ministry to receive their theological education at Saumar or Geneva, "from whence," says Heylin, "they returned well seasoned with the leaven of Calvinism."

Such an arrangement as this was extremely distasteful to the Archbishop; and, in order to draw the theological students to the English universities, he secured the endowment of several fellowships, by which their expenses could be provided for, and thus all excuse for going abroad would be removed.

The year 1638 is memorable in the annals of the English Church for the publication of Chillingworth's great work, "The Religion of Protestants a safe Way to Salvation." We are glad to know that Laud was his godfather, and that it was to his kind offices that the acute and active argumentative powers of this remarkable man were turned into the proper channel for rendering such essential service to the cause of truth.

Chillingworth, at one time, was a dupe to the artifices of the Jesuit Fisher, with whom our readers are already acquainted, and was persuaded by him to seek for light amidst the mazes of scepticism in the Romish college at Douay. Laud, who was then Bishop of London, hearing of the peril of his godson, determined that it should not be his fault if he were ensnared in the toils of Romanism. He therefore wrote to Chillingworth, entreating him to return to England, and to avail himself of the rare advantages to be found at the University of Oxford, to prosecute inquiries so interesting and important. The advice of the faithful godfather was followed, and the result is well known. Four years afterwards Chillingworth published the masterpiece of controversy, to which we have already referred, and lived and died a zealous defender of the English Church.

The next event of much importance in the life of Laud was his attempt to enforce the law for the suppression of dangerous and fanatical publications. In July, 1637, by his advice, a decree had been passed by the Star Chamber for controlling the unbridled license of the press. By this edict no book was allowed to be printed without permission of the Archbishop or the Bishop of London, or their chaplains, or of the Chancellor or Vice-Chancellor of the universities.

Of course such a decree was liable to abuse, and no doubt many improper things were done under its protection; but Laud thought that the safety of the Church depended upon its rigid enforcement, and he spared no pains to have its provisions carried into effect. The Puritans of that day were very fond of a Geneva edition of the Bible, with notes, which taught such doctrines as these: that kings might be disobeyed, and even murdered, if they were *idolaters;* that no promise was binding when, by the breaking of it, the interests of evangelical religion could be promoted; and that bishops were no better than the locusts of the Apocalypse that come up out of the pit.

The King and the Archbishop did not consider such *Bible notes* as the best possible devotional reading for the people, and they therefore wished to prevent the circulation of the book. James I. had forbidden that these commentaries should be printed in his dominions; but this prohibition was virtually set aside by importing an edition from Holland which had been published for the benefit of the English Non-conformists. This course was continued during the reign of Charles. Laud finally could endure it no longer; and having received intelligence that a fresh edition of the pernicious commentary was ready to be brought over, he was prepared to meet this importation of mischief with the terms of the royal decree.

The Puritans were greatly exasperated; and the Archbishop had added another to his long list of offences, for which he was soon to be brought to account. The clamors of the seditious, both in England and Scotland, were loudly assailing him, and the poor man could have enjoyed but few moments of uninterrupted peace.

One pleasant June morning in 1639, while the Archbishop was on his way to the court to attend upon the Queen, he was met by the Lord Mayor of London, who handed him two papers, — the one addressed to the chief magistrate himself and the aldermen of the city, the other exciting the apprentices against Laud. Both documents were signed by John Lilburn, a very fierce and turbulent man, who held the same views with Prynne and his associates, and who was equally bold in maintaining them. He had already been punished by order of the Star-Chamber, and this had only made him the more desperate. The voice of this determined Puritan, uttering imprecations upon the head of Laud, should have taught him how odious he had rendered himself to many who sympathized with Lilburn; and that fines and ear-cropping and imprisonment were not the best modes of building up the Church.

One of the things most generally complained of was that Laud had sent a circular letter to the bishops, in January, 1639, calling upon them and their clergy to contribute liberally towards the necessities of the King, who was then raising troops to punish the unruly Scots. The patriots seemed to forget that he had done this in obedience to the command of the Privy Council, and perhaps they never knew how long and earnestly he had labored for peace, even when every other councillor was opposed to him.

That he really did this, appears from a letter which he wrote in April of that year, to the Helvetic Pastors and Professors, in reply to an address he had received from them, lamenting the preparations for war.

Having first enlarged on the obduracy of the insurgents, the scandal which their outrageous proceedings might bring upon the name of the Reformation, and the cordial anxiety of the King to conciliate them by all concessions not ruinously inconsistent with his honor, he continues thus: "You have been prompted by your friendly affection towards our country (an affection not recently conceived, but derived from your forefathers,) to appeal to me; you adjure me, by all the miseries and perils of intestine war, to consult the peace of my conscience and the glory of my name, and to labor that the quarrel might not be brought to the decision of the sword, but be settled by the authority and the clemency of our King. You implore that I would be pleased to effect all this! I beseech of you, brethren, not to entertain bitter thoughts concerning me. I protest that, if it depended on my will, the thing would instantly be done. I call God to witness, and his anointed servant our King, and all of his Privy Council who have been present at our deliberations, that, in private and in public, I have uniformly been the friend of pacific measures. Nay, almost alone and unsupported, I have wrestled with our King, both by arguments and by prayers. And so far did I succeed, that he was prevailed upon, not only once or twice, but repeatedly, to offer to his rebellious people every condition of peace which a monarch could honorably concede or subjects could reasonably or rightfully demand. From them, however, he has been able to obtain nothing. It seems as if the gorgon's head had looked upon them, and turned them into stone. And yet, even now, I desist not from my purpose. My desire, at this moment, is for peace; and so would my voice be also, if our adversaries were not inflexibly set against it. And what, I would ask, in difficulties like these, can be accomplished by my weakness; seeing that we have to do with men that will either have no peace, or such a peace as no kingly majesty can endure? If, in the mean time, any one has reported me to you as an enemy to peace, (for I know how inveterately I am hated by each faction,) I beseech of Almighty God to have mercy upon him, and to bestow patience upon me."

This remarkable letter was sent with the entire approbation of the King. Indeed, we cannot doubt that at heart Charles desired peace, and that he was only aroused to the necessity of an appeal to arms, by the indignities heaped upon his authority.

"It has been thought by many, (remarks Mr. Le Bas,) that if the royal army had been faithfully conducted, and promptly marched into the heart of the country, the rebellious spirit of the Scots might have been speedily subdued. But the King's merciful and indecisive temper made him averse from all sanguinary extremities. Unfortunately, too, his fondness for magnificence and *feudalism* betrayed him into the pernicious resolution of calling his nobility about him, to his camp. This was a proceeding which proved most fatal to his interests by laying open many of the English Lords to the crafty and seductive representations of the Scots. The end of these infatuated counsels was the miserable pacification of June, 1639, which dismissed the rebels without punishment, grievously impaired the honor of his Majesty, discouraged all his truly wise and faithful servants, and imparted confidence to those who neither loved his person nor were attached to his service.

The notice of this disgraceful and "hollow truce," in the Diary of the Archbishop, is closed with the following prayer: — "God make it safe and honorable to the King and Kingdom:" a petition which could hardly have been accomplished without a miracle! Instead of safety and honor, it produced nothing but disaster and humiliation. The council was involved in perpetual and anxious debate on the most hopeful measures of deliverance. At these deliberations, Laud, of course, assisted. But, again, he protests that no clandestine advice was offered by him to his sovereign; that his sentiments were always openly delivered by him, in the hearing of his colleagues at the board; and that his counsels were never more violent than theirs. Still the cry went forth that he was the grand incendiary, and that all the impending calamities were the result of his overbearing and destructive influence. At length, the difficulties began to thicken so rapidly that the Archbishop joined Lord Strafford and the Marquess of Hamilton in proposing that a Parliament should be called as the only imaginable resource against probable ruin and confusion. At the same time, it was determined, that if, after all, the Commons should prove unmanageable, a resort to unusual means of supply would become inevitable. The language in which this advice is recorded by the Archbishop was unfortunate enough. "A resolution," he says, "was voted to assist the King, in extraordinary ways, if the Parliament should prove *peevish* and *refuse*." These words were afterwards made public, when the Archbishop's private journal was seized, among his other papers, in the Tower; and the unhappy phrase "peevish," was of itself atrociously treasonable in the majestic ears of the Long Parliament!"

CHAPTER FIFTEENTH.

The Short Parliament — Loud Complaints against the Bishops — Indirect Assault upon the Church — The King's Perplexities — Sir Henry Vane accomplishes a good deal of Mischief — "Hunting William the Fox" — A Mob assaults Lambeth Palace — The Ringleader hung — Charles pursues a singular Course in Regard to the Convocation — The Session continued — Seventeen New Canons — Bishop Goodman suspected of Romanism — Another Parliament called — The Scots Victorious — The Archbishop's Ruin predicted — Strafford accused of High Treason — Laud's turn comes next — A Solemn Service in his Private Chapel.

PARLIAMENT met on the 13th of April, 1640. Charles had managed to get along eleven years without holding one; but now his treasury was exhausted, — and he had tried all the expedients for replenishing it which unscrupulous tyranny could devise. Parliament opened, and loud complaints were made by the Covenanters against the Bishops. Their real object was to attack the throne, but they felt that this could most effectually be done by making a fierce assault upon the Church. They, therefore, began to proclaim aloud that the reformed religion never could be safe while the Bishops and other dignitaries of the Church were permitted to hold their offices undisturbed.

The rebellion was becoming daily more fierce and insolent, and no efforts were made for its suppression. The King was alarmed and perplexed, and knew not what next to do. In the midst of all this confusion and uncertainty, Sir Henry Vane, the elder, who was then Secretary of State, assured Charles that it was all folly for him to expect that means would be supplied to subdue the Scots, — and in consequence of this false, and, as some believe, treacherous information, his Majesty dissolved the Short Parliament on the 5th of May. The King soon afterwards discovered how grossly he had been deceived, but it was then too late to recall his hasty and fatal command.

Poor Laud, as usual, had to suffer for the faults of others; and the whole guilt of the transaction was ascribed to him.* A few days after the dissolution of Par-

* It is so much a matter of course that the lives of Cromwell and his associates should contain nothing but the most unfavorable views in regard to Laud's character, that we have been gratified to find so fair an estimate as the following, from the pen of Mr. J. T. Headley : — "Laud has probably been as much maligned as Cromwell. He was a bigot; so were many of the Puritans, fanatics. The former persecuted the dissenters, so did the latter the papists. Laud hurried men before the star-chamber and court of high-commission, and had them punished for no crime but that of speaking against oppression; nay, caused them to be put in the stocks, publicly whipped, and their ears cropped off; — equally violent measures were adopted by the Puritans against the Irish [Roman] Catholics. Now, to allow for the intolerance of the one, and not for that of the other, is manifestly unjust. The age and the times in which men live, must be taken into consideration when we judge of their characters. Laud was, doubtless, a sincere and honest prelate. He did what he thought was for the good of the church. Believing that it could not prosper in the midst of dissensions and radicalism, he set about their eradication in the way he thought best to secure his object. That he should see nothing but discord and ruin in the spirit of rebellion against the church and the state that was abroad, was natural. There was no more bigotry in his looking upon dissenters as criminals, than in the Puritans regarding the papists as such. Thus, while we regard his career as

liament, papers were scattered about the streets to excite the populace, containing invitations for the apprentices and others to assemble in St. George's Fields, "to hunt William the Fox, for breaking up the Parliament." A mob of several hundred ruffians assembled by night, and made an attack on Lambeth Palace, and threatened to tear the Archbishop in pieces. Laud had heard of their design beforehand, and had fortified the doors and windows as securely as he could; but the spirit manifested by the assailants was so determined, that the King obliged him to take up his quarters in the palace at Whitehall for several nights after this alarming demonstration. The insurrection was not quelled until the ringleader had been seized and executed.

Before the end of the Parliament, the Convocation had voted quite a large sum for the King, to be paid in six years, by

mad and foolish in the extreme, we see in it nothing so inconsistent as many do. His cruelties and persecutions indicate the weak bigot, rather than the unfeeling oppressor." — *Headley's Cromwell*, page 88.

equal annual portions. As soon as the dissolution was announced, the Archbishop sent word to the Convocation that their session should also be brought to a close, forgetting, in the excitement of the moment, that this could not be done without the King's consent. As soon as he was reminded of this, he asked Charles to give him the writ which was requisite, when, much to his astonishment, the King replied, that he wished the Convocation to continue in session until they had completed their grant of money, and finished certain church laws which were then under consideration.

The Archbishop was thus placed in very awkward circumstances, and although he doubted whether the measure proposed was either lawful or expedient, he was unable to change his Majesty's determination. The only satisfaction allowed him was, that he had permission to submit the question to the judgment of the Lord-Keeper and the Crown-Lawyers. The answer received from these authorities was, that "the Convocation, being called by the King's writ, under the Great Seal, doth continue, until it be dissolved by writ or commission under the Great Seal, *notwithstanding the Parliament be dissolved.*"

The Convocation, accordingly, continued to hold its sessions until the 29th of May, which allowed them time to finish the business which the King thought so important. Seventeen canons were formed for the better government of the church, and for the promotion of peace. All of the members of Convocation voted for them, with the exception of Dr. Goodman, Bishop of Gloucester, who had long been suspected of a leaning towards Romanism. He now confirmed this impression in the minds of many by telling Laud that he would sooner be torn by wild horses than subscribe the canon for suppressing the growth of Popery.

At first, the new church laws were quite popular; but within a month, the current changed, and they were as much abused as they had previously been commended.

Once more, the unfortunate Archbishop had to stand as a mark to be fired upon from every quarter. The course which he had pursued in regard to Bishop Goodman should have convinced his enemies that he was no friend to Romanism, however indiscreet he might be in taking so active a part in politics.

The life of Archbishop Laud is so closely interwoven with English history, that we must note the course of public events in order to continue the narrative. Although the King was well convinced that he had been betrayed by Vane, it was useless, now, to lament his own rash act in dissolving Parliament, and he determined to have recourse to voluntary loans of money, and to raise an army without delay. Within three weeks' space, £300,000 were paid into the royal treasury, — troops were enlisted and placed under the command of the Earl of Northumberland, with Strafford as Lieutenant-General, and Lord Conway as Master of the Horse.

Northumberland's illness obliged Strafford to hasten his march northward, and before he could reach his destination the battle of Newbury had been fought, and the victorious Scots were in possession of Newcastle. Strafford was far from being well himself, and not having full confidence in the loyalty of his soldiers, he did not think it prudent to venture to give battle, but retired to York, where the King had already arrived. Here a Council of Peers was held, and it was determined to call another Parliament, which assembled on the 3d of November, 1640. The times were most unpropitious. Law and order were alike despised; the fanaticism of the people was at its height; riots had broken out in London; seditious papers were scattered about, urging an attack upon Laud, and plots were laid for his assassination. Everybody predicted his ruin when the Parliament assembled, and he records, almost as if he accepted the omen, that on going into his study, October 27th, he found his picture fallen on its face lying upon the floor. But the old man did not quail nor falter. He took his place in Parliament, and preached before the Convocation, urging all to remain firm and faithful.

The House of Commons soon showed what they intended to do.

On the 11th of November, Strafford was accused of high treason, and on the 16th of December, the canons were condemned, as being against the King's prerogative, the laws of the realm, and the liberty of the people. The next blow fell on Archbishop Laud. On the 1st of December, Mr. D. Hollis, in the name of the people of England, accused William, Lord Archbishop of Canterbury, of high treason, and prayed he might be committed to safe custody, promising at a convenient time to specify the charges. The Archbishop was ordered to withdraw ; he craved leave to speak, and expressed his sorrow at such a charge being made against an innocent man. He was rudely interrupted by Lord Essex, browbeaten by Lord Say, and finally committed to the charge of Mr. J. Maxwell, the Usher of the Black Rod.

The following prayer was composed by Laud on this occasion: —

"O eternal God and merciful Father, I humbly beseech Thee, look down upon me in this time of my great and grievous affliction. Lord, if it be Thy blessed will, make mine innocency to appear, and free both me and my profession from all scandal thus raised upon me. And howsoever, if Thou be pleased to try me to the uttermost, I humbly beseech Thee, give me full patience, proportionable comfort, contentment with whatsoever Thou sendest, and an heart ready to die for Thy honor, the King's happiness, and this Church's preservation. And my zeal to these is all the sin (human frailty excepted) which is yet known to me in this particular for which I thus suffer. Lord, look upon me in mercy, and for the merits of Jesus Christ, pardon all my sins many and great, which have drawn down this judgment upon me, and then in all things do with me as seems best in Thine own eyes; and make me not only patient under, but thankful for whatsoever Thou dost, O Lord, my strength and my Redeemer. Amen."

With difficulty the Archbishop obtained leave to return to Lambeth to arrange his papers. And when at the hour of evening prayer he entered the chapel he had so piously restored, it may be that a saddened feeling came over him as he gazed upon its fair beauty for the last time. But God was with His servant, — and the service of the day carried with it consolation; and as the choir wafted in melodious strains the inspired words, "The floods are risen, O Lord, the floods have lift up their waves. The waves of the sea are mighty, and rage horribly; but yet the Lord, Who dwelleth on high, is mightier." Or, "Blessed is the man whom Thou chastenest, O Lord; and teachest him in Thy law." Or, "In the multitude of the sorrows I had in my heart, Thy comforts have refreshed my soul. They gather them together against the soul of the righteous, and condemn the innocent blood; but the Lord is my refuge, and my God is the strength of my confidence. He shall recompense them their wickedness, and destroy them in their own malice ; yea, the Lord our God shall destroy them." Every word of those evening Psalms spoke comfort; and the voice of the Prophet, in the first lesson, had its own message.

"For the Lord God will help me; therefore shall I not be confounded; therefore have I set my face like a flint, and I know that I shall not be ashamed."

"He is near that justifieth me; who will contend with me? Let us stand together; who is mine adversary? Let him come near to me."

"Behold, the Lord God will help me; who is he that shall condemn me? Lo, they all shall wax old as a garment; the moth shall eat them up."

"Who is among you that feareth the Lord, that obeyeth the voice of His servant; that walketh in darkness and hath no light? Let him trust in the Name of the Lord, and stay upon his God."

"Behold, all ye that kindle a fire, that compass yourselves about with sparks; walk in the light of your fire, and in the sparks that ye have kindled. This shall ye have of Mine hand; ye shall lie down in sorrow."

And the chief of the apostles, too, seemed to speak to him, and remind him that he must shortly put off this tabernacle; and so the service closed. The organ ceased,— the chant died away,—the closing prayer was said;—one last look the prelate cast upon the fair altar he had raised, the glowing windows he had restored,—and then, at eventide took boat, and amid the blessings of his poorer neighbors, who crowded the portal and loudly prayed for his safe return, departed to his prison-house. And so great an impression did that service make upon his mind, that ever after till the day of his death, the psalms 93 and 94, which were then sung, were recited by him daily.

CHAPTER SIXTEENTH.

Uncertainty of Human Greatness — Confidence in God — Ten weary Weeks — Ballads and Caricatures — Articles of Impeachment brought in — Laud's Reply — His Removal to the Tower — Advised to escape Strafford's Fate — " My Lord, your Prayers and your Blessing " — The Archbishop's Illness — His Courage and Patience unsubdued — The King's unprincipled Conduct — The Bishops sent to the Tower — " No Bishops ! "—The Broken Leg — " Curse ye, Meroz " ! — Seeking the Lord in Trouble.

ALAS! for the uncertainty of all human greatness, — the Archbishop of Canterbury was now the inmate of a prison, — and completely in the power of those who so heartily desired his ruin. There, in darkness and solitude, we find the venerable prelate upon his knees, communing with that gracious FATHER who never forsakes His children in their afflictions. "O Lord, cast me not off in the time of mine age," is his earnest supplication; "forsake me not, O God, in mine old age, now I am gray-headed, until I have declared Thy strength unto this generation, and Thy power to all them that are to come. Amen.

"O Lord, though Thou hast shortened the days of my youth, yet cover me not with dishonor. Hide not Thyself from me forever, but remember how short my time is, and make me remember it, O Lord. Amen.

"O Lord, teach me to number my days, that I may apply my heart unto wisdom. Amen.

"O Lord, hide not Thy face from me in the time of trouble, for my days are consumed away like smoke, and my bones are burnt up like a firebrand. My days are gone like a shadow, and I am withered like grass. Thou, O Lord, has brought down my strength in my journey, and shortened my days. But, O God, take me not away, but in the timeliness of my age, that I may continue to serve Thee and be faithful to Thy service, till Thou remove me hence. Amen.

"O Lord, have mercy upon me, and bring my soul out of prison, that I may give thanks unto Thy Name, even in Jesus Christ our Lord. Amen.

"O Lord, blessed is the man that hath Thee for his help, and whose hope is in Thee. O Lord, help me and all them to right that suffer wrong. Thou art the Lord which looseth men out of prison,—which helpeth them that are fallen. O Lord, help and deliver me when and as it shall seem best to Thee, even for Jesus Christ His sake. Amen.

"O Lord, Thine indignation lies hard upon me; and though Thou hast not (for Thy mercy is great) vexed me with all Thy storms, yet Thou hast put my acquaintance far from me, and I am so fast in prison that I cannot get forth. Lord, I call daily upon Thee, hear and have mercy, for Jesus Christ His sake. Amen."

Laud's old enemy, Williams, was set at

liberty, and, in order to please the people, the King nominated this subtle man as Archbishop of York.

Ten weary weeks passed by, and the aged prisoner — now nearly seventy — remained at Maxwell's, in charge of the Black Rod, — a large sum being demanded of him every day to defray the expenses of his own imprisonment. During this time, the members of Parliament were busily engaged in raking up every action or word of his past life which could possibly be turned against him, — while the town was filled with scurrilous ballads on his person and office, and absurd caricatures in the shape of coarse wood-cuts. One of the last represented the unfortunate prelate as confined in a cage, and fastened with a chain. His only remark on the subject was, "I thank God He made me patient, and God forgive them."

His enemies thought, at one time, of sending him out of the country without a trial, but it was finally determined to bring him into open court. On the 26th of February, 1641, fourteen articles were presented against him, by Sir H. Vane, as follows: —

1. That the Archbishop had traitorously endeavored to subvert the fundamental laws of the Realm, and to persuade the King that he might levy money, without the consent of Parliament.

2. That he had encouraged sermons and publications tending to the establishment of arbitrary power.

3. That he had interrupted and perverted the course of justice at Westminster Hall.

4. That he had traitorously and corruptly sold justice; and advised the King to sell judicial and other offices.

5. That he had surreptitiously caused a pernicious Book of Canons to be published without lawful authority; and had unlawfully enforced subscription to it.

6. That he had assumed a Papal and tyrannical power, both in ecclesiastical and temporal matters.

7. That he had labored to subvert God's true religion, and to introduce Popish superstition and idolatry.

8. That he had usurped the nomination to many ecclesiastical benefices, and had promoted none but persons who were Popishly affected, or otherwise unsound in doctrine, or corrupt in manners.

9. That he had committed the licensing of books to chaplains notoriously disaffected to the Reformed religion.

10. That he had endeavored to reconcile the Church of England to the Church of Rome; had held intelligence with Jesuits and the Pope; and had permitted a Popish hierarchy to be established in this Kingdom.

11. That he had silenced many godly ministers; hindered the preaching of God's word; cherished profaneness and ignorance; and caused many of the King's subjects to forsake the country.

12. That he had endeavored to raise discord between the Church of England

and other Reformed Churches; and had oppressed the Dutch and French Congregations in England.

13. That he had labored to introduce innovations in religion and government, into the Kingdom of Scotland; and to stir up war between the two countries.

14. That, to preserve himself from being questioned for these traitorous practices, he had labored to divert the ancient course of Parliamentary proceeding, and to incense the King against all Parliaments."

When these charges had been read, Laud received permission to say a few words in reply. He availed himself of this privilege, — and addressed the House of Lords to this effect: —

"His charge was," he said, "great and heavy. He should, indeed, be unworthy to live, if it could be made good. It denounced him as an enemy to God, in point of religion; to the King, in point of allegiance; to the public, in point of safety. The King, it was true, was but little named in the impeachment; but, he held the civil and political union of King and people to be so intimate, that no man could be faithful to the one and yet treacherous to the other. Heavy, however, as his accusation was, he was unable, as yet, correctly to estimate the entire weight of it. At present, it dealt merely in general charges. But he trusted that, when his accusers should enter into proof of each particular complaint, his innocence would furnish him with a sufficient answer. He might, indeed, have fallen into errors; but these, he hoped, would meet with an indulgent construction from their lordships. The affairs which had passed through his hands had been of great variety and moment; such as might easily betray far abler men than himself into occasional mistake. With regard to the charge of corruption in his office, he blessed God that he feared no accuser that would speak the truth. But that which moved him most was that he should be deemed foul and false in the profession of his religion; that he should be thought to have his heart at Rome, while his lips were with the Church of England; that he should be suspected of laboring, with secret and treacherous craft, to bring back the superstitions of Rome upon his country. This, he confessed, did most exceedingly trouble him. And if he should chance to forget himself, and fall into passion when speaking of it, his case would but resemble that of St. Jerome, who declared that he knew not how to be patient when arraigned of falsehood in religion; and this was said by Jerome upon infinitely less provocation than that which was now laid upon *him:* for he (the Archbishop) was charged, not only with the baseness of personal defection, but with a design to involve the whole nation in apostasy. He then proceeded to enlarge upon those parts of the impeachment which contained this falsehood, and so concluded an address which ought to have covered his accusers with confusion."

It was determined that the Archbishop should now be removed to the Tower, — but, at his request, he was allowed to remain at his present lodgings until the following Monday, the 1st of March. During his confinement at Maxwell's, his gentleness and patience had so completely won for him the good opinion of the keeper's wife, that she used afterwards to declare that he was the most excellent and pious soul she had ever known.

On the day appointed for his transfer to the Tower, Laud was conveyed to the place of his last imprisonment, at noon, — the hour when most of the citizens would be at dinner, — in order that he might escape observation and insult. But these precautions were of no avail; a clamor was begun by a few apprentices, and the tumult grew louder and louder, until it became so outrageous that Maxwell himself was moved with grief and indignation; — while the poor prisoner meekly said, "I bless God for it, my patience was not moved; I looked upon a higher cause than the tongues of Shimei and his children."

He was now safe in the Tower, and there he was left for many months to "the great weakening," says he, "of my aged body and waste of my poor fortune; whereas all that I do desire, is a just and fair trial, with such an issue, better or worse, as it shall please God to give." While he was thus confined, the great oriental scholar, Pocock, whom he had employed to travel and collect manuscripts in the East, returned to England, and with a becoming sense of gratitude and duty, waited upon his patron in prison. He delivered him a message from Hugo Grotius, himself at that time a fugitive, having been driven from his country by the Calvinistic party. Grotius entreated him to make his escape, if possible, and cross the sea, there to preserve himself for better times, or at least to obtain security from the malice of his enemies and the rage of a deluded people.

The lord-keeper, and one of the principal secretaries, had already taken this course. Laud, however, without hesitation, answered that he could not comply with his friend's advice.

"An escape," said he, "is feasible enough; yea, 'tis, I believe, the very thing my enemies desire, for every day an opportunity for it is presented, a passage being left free in all likelihood for this purpose, that I should endeavor to take the advantage of it. But they shall not be gratified by me. I am almost seventy years old; shall I now go about to prolong a miserable life by the trouble and shame of flying? And were I willing to go, whither should I fly? Should I go into France, or any other Popish country, it would give some seeming grounds to that charge of popery, which they have endeavored, with so much industry and so little reason, to fasten upon me. But if I should get into Holland, I should expose myself to the insults of those sectaries there, to whom my character is odious, and have every Anabaptist come and pull me by the beard. No; I am resolved not to think of flight; but patiently to expect and bear what a good and wise Providence hath provided for me, of what kind soever it shall be."

Orders were given that he should not be permitted to see Strafford; and this order was enforced, even when Strafford, on the night before his execution, requested the lieutenant of the Tower that, if it were possible, he might speak with the Archbishop, saying, "You shall hear what passeth between us, for it is not a time now either for him to plot heresy, or me to plot treason." The lieutenant answered, that he was bound by his orders, and advised him to petition Parliament for that favor.

"No," replied Strafford; "I have gotten my despatch from them, and will trouble them no more. I am now petitioning a Higher Court, where neither partiality can be expected nor error feared." Then turning to Usher, the Primate of Ireland, he said, "My Lord, I will tell you what I should have spoken to my Lord's Grace of Canterbury. You shall desire the Archbishop to lend me his prayers this night, and to give me his blessing when I do go abroad to-morrow; and to be in his window, that by my last farewell I may give him thanks for this and all his other former favors."

When Usher delivered this mournful message, Laud replied, that in conscience he was bound to the first, and in duty and obligation to the second; but he feared weakness and passion would not lend him eyes to behold his last departure.

"The next morning," says Laud, "as he past by, he turned towards me and took the solemnest leave that I think was ever, by any at distance, taken one of another."

Solemn indeed it was, beyond all example; for Strafford halted before the window, and when his old and venerable friend came to it, bowed himself to the ground and said, "My Lord, your prayers and your blessing!" Laud lifted up his hands and bestowed both, and then, overcome with grief, fell to the ground senseless; while Strafford, bowing himself a second time, said, "Farewell, my Lord, God protect your innocency!" When the Primate recovered his senses, he said, as if fearing that what had passed might be deemed an unmanly and unbecoming weakness, he trusted, by God's assistance, that when he should come to his own execution, the world would perceive he had been more sensible of Lord Strafford's fate than of his own."*

Laud's distress of mind at the death of his friend, brought on a severe illness, — and a prison was a comfortless place for one under such painful circumstances. His trust in God, however, never failed him, as these extracts from his Devotions will show: —

* *Southey's Book of the Church*, Chapter XVII.

"O Lord, the sorrows of death compass me, and the snares of it are ready to overtake me. When Thou wilt dissolve my tabernacle, Thou alone knowest; therefore in this my trouble I will call upon Thee my Lord, and will complain unto my God. O be with me at the instant of my death, and receive me, for Jesus Christ His sake. Amen.

"O Lord, the snares of death compass me round about, the pains of hell get hold upon me. I have found trouble and heaviness, but will call upon Thy name, O Lord; O Lord deliver my soul. Deliver my soul from death, mine eyes from tears, and my feet from falling, that I may walk before Thee in the land of the living. Amen.

"There is no health in my flesh by reason of Thy wrath, neither is there any rest in my bones by reason of my sin; yet, O Lord, be merciful unto me, and heal me, even for Thy Name's sake. Amen.

"O Lord, I give Thee humble and

hearty thanks for the great and almost miraculous bringing of me back from the bottom of my grave. What Thou hast further for me to do or to suffer, Thou alone knowest. Lord, give me patience and courage, and all Christian resolution to do Thee service, and grace to do it. And let me not live longer than to honor Thee, through Jesus Christ. Amen."

Charles, with his usual selfishness, abandoned his poor friend to his fate; and with equal inconsistency, set out for Scotland, leaving the Church at the mercy of her enemies. Advantage was immediately taken of his absence, to make various changes to suit Puritan notions; and growing bolder as they advanced, the Commons committed the Archbishop of York and eleven Bishops to the Tower, for having signed an ill-advised protestation against the legality of the Parliamentary proceedings in their absence from the House of Lords, — the violence of the rabble having rendered their progress thither impossible. This was

December 30th, 1641. On January 4th, 1642, Charles made his ineffectual attempt to seize the five members. How sorely must he have missed Strafford! The great Earl would have dragged them from any hiding-place, but Charles alone was no match for a Puritan Parliament.

The cry was now for no Bishops, and Saturday, February 6th, 1642, the bill abolishing the Episcopal votes in Parliament was passed. Laud carefully noted all proceedings from his prison, the rigor of which does not seem to have been increased, though he was not allowed to communicate with his brother Prelates. His jurisdiction was next sequestered; he was ordered to refer his patronage for approval to the Commons; and traps were laid to ensnare him into admissions fatal to his cause, — but he was on his guard, and foiled their machinations.

An additional trial also befell him. He broke the sinew of his leg where it had been injured before, and was confined two months to his room. He was thus cut off from the public worship of God, — a great deprivation to him; but May 15th "made shift between his man and his staff, to go to Church." The preacher so far forgot Christian charity and common courtesy as to preach a violent invective against him, from Judges v. 23: "Curse ye Meroz, said the angel of the Lord," so that the women and boys, he said, stood up in the Church to look at him. I humbly thank God for my patience, he adds. On which side Christianity and the spirit of the Gospel were, with Laud or this fanatical party, whose powers of abuse have always been remarkable, let the subjoined extract from his devotions testify:

"If I find favor in Thine eyes, O Lord, Thou wilt bring me again, and show me both the ark and the tabernacle, and set me right in Thy service, and make me joyful and glad in Thee. But if Thou say, (O, for Jesus His sake, say it *not*,) I have no pleasure in thee; behold, here

I am, do with me as seemeth good in Thine own eyes. Amen.

"O Lord, whatsoever Thou shalt lay upon me, I will hold my peace, and not open my mouth, because it is Thy doing and my deserving. Amen.

"O Lord Almighty, O God of Israel, the soul that is in trouble, and the spirit that is vexed, crieth unto Thee. Hear, O Lord, and have mercy, for Thou art merciful, and have pity upon me, because I have sinned before Thee, for Thou endurest forever; but unless Thou have mercy I utterly perish. Have mercy, therefore, even for Jesus Christ His sake. Amen.

"Gracious Father, the life of man is a warfare upon earth, and the dangers which assault us are diversely pointed against us. I humbly beseech Thee, be present with me in all the course and passages of my life; but especially in the services of my calling. Suffer no malice to be able to hurt me, no cunning to circumvent me, no violence to oppress me, no falsehood to betray me. That which I cannot foresee, I beseech Thee prevent; that which I cannot withstand, I beseech Thee master; that which I do not fear, I beseech Thee unmask and frustrate; that being delivered from all danger, both of soul and body, I may praise Thee, the Deliverer, and see how happy a thing it is to make the Lord of Hosts my Helper in the day of fear and trouble. Especially, O Lord, bless and preserve me at this time from, &c., that I may glorify Thee for this deliverance also, and be safe in the merits and the mercies of Jesus Christ my only Lord and Saviour. Amen.

"O Lord, Thou hast fed me with the bread of affliction, and given me plenty of tears to drink. I am become a very strife to my neighbors; and mine enemies laugh me to scorn. But turn Thee again, Thou God of Hosts; show me the light of Thy countenance, and I shall be whole. Amen.

CHAPTER SEVENTEENTH.

Long and cruel Confinement — Carrying Measures with a high Hand — An early Visitor, and not a very welcome One — Death of an old and faithful Servant — The Members of Parliament sign the Covenant — Ten New Articles of Impeachment — Adding Insult to Injury — The Trial begins — Indignities and Insults — The Charge of Treason not sustained — Reluctant Compliment from Prynne — To be condemned in Spite of the Law — Hard Names — Christmas kept as a Fast — Refinement of Cruelty — Laud and the Church perish together.

ARCHBISHOP LAUD had been committed to prison on charge of high treason, in 1640; but so cruel and unrelenting were his enemies, that he was not brought to trial until 1643. Meanwhile, England had been laid waste by that sad war, for particulars of which we must refer our readers to the historians of those times. The two Houses of Parliament were carrying measures with a high hand. Having got Laud out of the way, they voted that the offices of Archbishop, Bishops, and other dignitaries of the Church, should be done away with, and quietly took possession of their revenues. Laud was stripped of everything he had, and as those who kept him in confinement refused to help him, he was dependent for his daily bread upon the charity of friends.

On the last day of May, 1643, his inveterate adversary, William Prynne, entered his room at the Tower, while he was still in bed, and examined his pockets, and laid hands on all the papers he could find, — and among them were those which the Archbishop had prepared for his defence. The rough Puritan, who had by no means forgotten the cropping of his ears some years before, even deprived the Archbishop of his book of private devotions. "He must needs see," says Laud, "what passed between God and me, — a thing, I think, scarce ever offered to any Christian. I was somewhat troubled to see myself used in this manner, but knew no help but in God and the patience which He had given me; and how His gracious providence over me, and His goodness to me, wrought upon all this, I shall in the end discover, and will magnify, however it succeed with me."

On the 23d of September, the Archbishop lost an old and faithful servant, Adam Torless, who had waited upon him for more than forty years,—a sad affliction, indeed, to one who had so few friends left.

Two days afterwards, "for the encouragement of the Scots," as it was said, but really because the Parliament had become alarmed at the King's successes, the covenant was taken in St. Margaret's Church by the House of Commons and the Assembly of Divines. Many of the Lords, Knights, gentlemen, and soldiers, living about London, soon followed their example, and Puritanism thus felt itself strong enough to go on with its work. By the 23d of October, ten new articles of impeachment were brought against Laud, to this effect: —

1. That the Archbishop had caused the dissolution of the Parliaments held in the 3d and 4th years of the King.

2. That he had labored to advance the authority of the Church, and the prerogative of the King, above the law.

3. That he had procured a stop to his majesty's writs of prohibition.

4. That he had caused execution of judgment to be staid, in favor of a clergyman, charged with non-residence.

5. That he had imprisoned Sir John Corbet for causing the Petition of Right to be read at the Quarter Sessions.

6. That he had suppressed the Corporation of Feoffees for buying impropriations.

7. That he had harbored several Popish Priests.

8. That he had averred that the Church could never be brought to conformity without a severer blow than had yet been struck.

9. That he had introduced an unlawful oath into the Canons.

10. That he had recommended extraordinary ways of supply, if the Parliament should prove *peevish.*

The next day the Archbishop received an order to present his answer to these charges, in writing, by the 30th of the month. He entreated that he might have more time for the purpose, which was granted; but when he asked that his papers might be restored to him, he was told that he could have copies made of them at his own expense, if he chose to do so. This was adding insult to injury, for his persecutors knew that they had robbed him of his property, and that he had not a penny even, with which to buy bread.

The trial began, in due form, on the 12th of March, 1644, and lasted until January of the following year.

We have not time to speak of all the indignities to which he was exposed during this long period of suspense. Prynne tampered with the witnesses, and common decency was constantly violated. Garbled extracts were produced from Laud's diary, and hasty words, which he had spoken at the council-table, were now repeated to swell the charges against him. All the arbitrary proceedings of the Star-Chamber were laid at his door. But, in spite of these strenuous efforts to prove him guilty of treason, the judges were obliged unanimously to declare that this grievous charge was not established.

Indeed, the Archbishop had vindicated himself against every accusation with such masterly ability, that even William Prynne reluctantly said, "To give him his due, he made as full, as gallant, and as pithy a defence of so bad a cause, and spake so much for himself, as it was possible for the wit of man to invent; and that, with so much art, sophistry, vivacity, oratory, audacity, and confidence, without the least blush or acknowledgment of guilt in anything — as argued him rather obstinate than innocent, impudent than penitent, a far better orator and sophister than Protestant or Christian; yea, a truer son of the Church of Rome than of the Church of England."

The Commons were greatly enraged at the prospect of their victim's escape; and finding that he could not be condemned according to law, they determined that he should suffer in spite of the law. They hardly thought that Charles could be induced to consent to his death, and therefore the plan was arranged that he should be condemned by an ordinance of both Houses of Parliament, without the approval of the King.

"It is a fundamental law of English liberty," says Heylin, commenting on these proceedings, "that no man shall be condemned or put to death but by the lawful judgment of his peers, or by the law of the land, *i. e.*, in the ordinary way of trial; and sure an ordinance of both Houses, without the royal assent, is no part of the law of England, nor held an ordinary way of trial.

So, all else failing, an ordinance was resolved on; but first, (November 11th and 13th,) they had him down to the bar of the House of Commons, and baited him with their lawyers, while the old man still defended himself with unusual vigor, so as even to extort the admiration of his implacable foes. He says: "I was exceeding faint with speaking so long, and I had great pain and soreness in my heart for almost a fortnight after; then, I thank God, it wore away."

The moment the prisoner was gone, they called for the ordinance, and voted him guilty of high treason; on Saturday, November 16th, they sent it to the Lords.

The Lords were in a difficulty. They had no good-will to Laud; but to put him to death in this way was establishing a very awkward precedent, which might easily be turned against themselves. They debated and debated, and put the matter off, notwithstanding Lord Pembroke pressed them to destroy the "rascal," "the villain," as he was courteously pleased to term the Metropolitan of England.

The Commons, too, were not behind in "urgency," and sent a message, bidding them agree to the ordinance, or "else the multitude would come down and force them to it." This threat aroused the fast ebbing spirit of the upper House, and their answer was worthy of English gentlemen. But, unfortunately, they contented themselves with words. When the crisis came, they lost heart, and voted the Archbishop, December 17th, guilty of the facts charged against him, and put it to the judges whether they amounted to treason. The judges unanimously replied, "No."

Here was a new difficulty for the Lords. On Christmas eve they desired a conference with the Commons, and said they could not find him guilty of treason by any law. They were simply bidden to pass the ordinance. Christmas-day, for the first time in the annals of Church history, was kept as a fast. The end was drawing on. The Commons in turn, January 2d, 1645, requested a conference, to satisfy the Lords in the matter of law. Of course none of Laud's counsel were present on this occasion, though all the parliamentary lawyers were; and it had the effect of satisfying the upper House. On January 2d, the ordinance condemning an Archbishop to the gibbet, passed the Lords, — that august assembly being represented by the Earls of Kent, Pembroke, Salisbury, Bolingbroke, and the Lords North and Grey of Wark. And so justice was once again dethroned, and law and equity superseded, at the bidding of the Commons of England.

But the day of retribution was at hand. Strafford had suffered death by an act of the three estates of the realm; two concurred in the sacrifice of Laud. But when these same men, abandoned more and more to a reprobate mind, stretched forth their hand against the King, there was but one estate left. The Lords had crouched to the Commons, and done their behests of blood; and, as their reward, were themselves destroyed by the very monster they had fostered. Retributive justice is often visible, even in this life.

Word was brought to the Archbishop on January 4th, that he was to die on the 10th, by hanging. He was not afraid to die, but he thought it only his duty to the sovereign he loved so well, and served so faithfully, to lay before the Houses a pardon which he had received from His Majesty, and which had been suggested by his friend Mr. Hyde. It was the only thing the King could do to show he loved him, and would try to save him; and though, as he expected, it was contemptuously rejected, it was nevertheless very soothing, as a token of Charles's affection.

His last hope gone, he petitioned that the mode of death might be altered to beheading, and that his chaplains, Dr. Sterne, Dr. Heywood, or Dr. Martin, might attend him. The

Lords granted both prayers; *the Commons refused both.* They afterwards relented so far as to alter the sentence to beheading; but they would not allow the attendance of Dr. Sterne, unless he were accompanied by Dr. Marshall or Mr. Palmer, two noted Puritans. They would not leave even the last moments of their victim in peace; they would tease him with controversy, and deprive him, all that lay in their power, of peace and comfort. There is something fiendish in such a refinement of cruelty. But he who was so soon to be a martyr, calmly and quietly set about his preparation, and meekly on his knees made his peace with God.

The same day that the Lords consented to the attainder, they also passed an ordinance that the Book of Common Prayer should be laid aside, and the form prepared by the Assembly of Divines be substituted. Laud lived, it would seem, only to protect the Church in his land. Her prosperity (so far as her outward establishment was affected) seemed bound up with the being of her chief pastor. If we may say that he died in her behalf, who would wish for a nobler testimony to the importance of the struggle he had maintained? Who would wish for a nobler fate? *

* Baines's Laud, pages 245, &c., with occasional abridgments and other alterations.

CHAPTER EIGHTEENTH.

A quiet Sleep before an eventful Day — Brutish Shouts and Mockings until the End — Parting Address to the People — Last Prayer — The Impertinence of Sir John Clotworthy — An Execrable Calumny exposed — All Hallows, Barking — Burial Service under peculiar Circumstances — Laud's Remains removed to Oxford — An American Traveller visits the Spot — Curious Relicts of the Past — Good out of Evil — The Fine Gold comes forth from the Furnace — Last Will and Testament.

On the evening before his execution, Archbishop Laud refreshed himself with a moderate meal, and having again poured out his soul in prayer, he retired to rest, and slept so soundly, that his attendants had to awake him when the fatal hour had come. It was a cold, dreary, winter morning,— January 10th, 1645,— a notable day, indeed, in the history of the Church.

The aged man at once arose, and continued in prayer until the officers arrived to conduct him to the scaffold. His request that his own chaplains might be with him at this trying hour was refused.* On his way to the place of execution, he was assailed by the brutal shouts and mockings of the lowest rabble,—who would not let the gray-haired Bishop go to his grave in peace. But he heeded them not; his thoughts were far away, above the scenes of this wicked world. With the buoyant step and cheerful countenance of one who was ascending a throne, he mounted the platform, and permission being given him to address the people, he read to them an address which he had prepared for the occasion.

In this address, he acknowledged that, although he felt the infirmities of flesh and blood, and might have been glad that the cup which was given him should pass from him, yet he was now ready to drink it. He then reminded his hearers, that, when God's servants were driven to enter the Red Sea,

* Although his enemies finally agreed that a clergyman should go with him, they spoiled even this small concession, by sending two of their fanatical teachers also.

their enemies were drowned in the pursuit. He was well assured that God was able, if it seemed good to Him, to deliver him, even as He delivered the three faithful ones from the fiery furnace. His resolution, too, was like theirs. He never would bow down before the image which the *people* had set up. Neither would he forsake the truth of God, as it were, to follow the bleating of Jeroboam's calves.

The people, he affirmed, were wretchedly misguided. He prayed that God, in his mercy, would open their eyes; for, now, the blind were leading the blind; and, if this should long continue to be so, both must fall into the ditch together. He knew that certain of his predecessors had been brought to a bloody grave. But he was now called upon to follow them by a path before untrodden. He was not only the first Archbishop, but the first man, in England, who had died by an *ordinance* of Parliament. He trusted, however, that his cause would appear, in heaven, with a complexion very different from that which had been given to it on earth.

He next observed, that our multiplied divisions had produced such a harvest to the Pope as had never been known in England since the Reformation. And he was deeply anxious to vindicate His Majesty from any share in fostering that pernicious growth. On my conscience, he said, I know him to be as guiltless of this charge as any man now living. I hold that he is as sound a Protestant, according to the religion by law established, as any man in his dominions; and that no one would more freely venture his life in defence of it.

Having, next, warned the people how fearful a thing it was to fall into the hands of the Living God, when He maketh inquisition for blood, he lamented the condition of the Church of England, which had become like an oak cleft into shivers with wedges made out of its own body; and, at every cleft, profaneness and irreligion rushing in.

He then proceeded to speak of himself;

"I was born and baptized," he says, "in the Church of England; in that profession I have ever since lived; and in that I come now to die. This is no time to dissemble with God; least of all in matters of religion. What clamors and slanders I have endured, for laboring to keep an uniformity in the external service of God, according to the doctrine and discipline of that Church, all men know, and I have abundantly felt.

"And now," he added, "I am accused of high treason; a crime which my soul abhors. I am charged with an endeavor to subvert the laws, and to overthrow the Protestant religion. In vain I protested my innocence of these crimes. The protestations of prisoners, it was said, could never be received at the bar of justice. I can bring no witness of my heart! I now, therefore, make my protest, in the presence of God, and his holy angels, that I never did attempt the subversion either of religion or of law.

"I further have been maligned, as an enemy to Parliaments. I know their uses too well to be their enemy. But I, likewise, know that Parliaments have been sometimes guilty of misgovernment and abuse; and that no corruption is so bad as the corruption of that which, in itself, is excellent. From the power of Parliaments there is no appeal. If, therefore, they should be guilty of oppression, the subject is left without all remedy.

"But I have done," he said, in conclusion. "I forgive all the world; all and every of those bitter enemies which have persecuted me. And I humbly desire to be forgiven — of God first; and then, of every man, whether I have offended him or not; if he do but conceive that I have, Lord, do thou forgive me, and I dq beg forgiveness of him. And so, I heartily bid you join in prayer with me."

He then fell on his knees, and uttered the following memorable supplication, no word ot which should be suffered to perish from the annals of martyrdom:

"O Eternal God and merciful Father! look down upon me in mercy, in the riches and fulness of all thy mercies, look down upon me; but not till Thou hast nailed my sins to the cross of Christ, not till Thou hast bathed me in the blood of Christ; not till I have hid myself in the wounds of Christ, that so the punishment due unto my sins may pass over me. And since Thou art pleased to try me to the utmost, I humbly beseech Thee, give me now in this great instant, full patience, proportionable comfort, and a heart ready to die for Thine honor, the King's happiness, and the Church's preservation. And my zeal to this (far from arrogancy be it spoken), is all the sin, (human frailty excepted, and all the incidents thereunto,) which is yet known to me in this particular, for which I now come to suffer; I say, in this particular of treason. But otherwise my sins are many and great; Lord, pardon them all; and those especially (whatever they are) which have drawn down this present judgment upon me! And when Thou hast given me strength to bear it, do with me as seems best in Thine own eyes;

and carry me through death, that I may look upon it, in what visage soever it shall appear to me.—Amen! And that there may be a stop of this issue of blood in this more than miserable kingdom, (I shall desire that I may pray for the people too, as well as for myself.) O Lord, I beseech Thee, give grace of repentance to all bloodthirsty people. But if they will not repent, O Lord, confound all their devices, defeat and frustrate all their designs and endeavors, upon them, which are or shall be contrary to the glory of Thy great name, the truth and sincerity of Religion, the establishment of the King and his posterity after him in their just rights and privileges, the honor and conservation of Parliaments in their just power, the preservation of this poor Church in her truth, peace, and patrimony, and the settlement of this distracted and distressed people under their ancient laws, and in their native liberty. And when Thou hast done all this in mere mercy to them, O Lord, fill their hearts with thankfulness, and with religious, dutiful obedience to Thee and

Thy commandments all their days—Amen. Lord Jesus—Amen,—and receive my soul into Thy bosom! Amen. Our Father which art in heaven, &c."

When he rose from his knees, he gave his papers to Sterne, the chaplain, and approached the block. On perceiving, through the crevices of the scaffold, that some persons were standing beneath, he calmly requested that they might be told not to remain under the block, as he did not wish his blood to fall upon them.

Some noisy, hard-hearted Puritans were so much surprised and vexed to see the hasty and impetuous Archbishop changed by the grace of God into a meek and patient sufferer, that they were unwilling that the last few moments of his life should be left undisturbed. Accordingly, Sir John Clotworthy, who had already distinguished himself by his outrageous violence against the Earl of Stafford, stepped forward, and with the utmost impertinence asked, "What is the comfortablest saying for a dying man to have in his mouth?"

"I desire to depart and to be with Christ," was Laud's answer.

"There must be a ground of assurance," continued Clotworthy.

"The assurance is to be found within, and no words can express it rightly," was the martyr's meek reply.

"It must be founded upon a word or place of sacred Scripture," pertinaciously urged his persecutor.

"That word is the Knowledge of Jesus," replied Laud. And wishing to be rid of this importunity, and to escape the malice which persecuted his last moments with controversy, he turned to the executioner, and without a change of muscle said, as he gave him money, "Here, honest friend, God forgive thee, and I do; do thy office with mercy."

Once more the Archbishop kneeled upon his knees and prayed to his God: "Lord, I am coming as fast as I can. I know I must pass through the shadow of death before I come to see Thee. But it is but *umbra mortis*, a mere shadow of death, a little darkness upon nature; but Thou by Thy merits and passion hast broken through the jaws of death. Lo, Lord, receive my soul, and have mercy upon me, and bless this kingdom with peace and plenty, and with brotherly love and charity, that there may not be this effusion of Christian blood amongst them, for Jesus Christ His sake, if it be Thy will."

He laid his head upon the block, and for a few moments he was silent, but his lips moved as in prayer. Once more he spake aloud: "Lord, receive my soul." It was the signal to the headsman. And so he died. The moment the head was severed from the body, an ashy paleness overspread the countenance of the deceased. The Archbishop was naturally of a florid complexion, and when his persecutors saw him ascend the scaffold with cheeks unblanched, they circulated the despicable falsehood, that he had painted his face, in order that he might die with the appearance of fortitude. The change which death produced in his complexion, exposed this execrable calumny.

Faithful men carried the body of the Archbishop to its resting-place, and it was laid in a vault at All Hallows, Barking,* near the Tower; and although a law had already been passed for the suppression of the Prayer-Book, the sublime service for the burial of the dead was performed over his remains.

It had always been Laud's earnest wish

* "The church of All-Hallows, Barking, happened to stand open, much to my satisfaction, as I was threading a very narrow and old-fashioned street near the Tower; and I entered, with a thrill of emotion, to behold the venerable interior, where the service for the burial of the dead was said over the bleeding corpse of Archbishop Laud, as it was brought in just after the axe had made him a martyr, and here temporarily interred. I remember that Southey remarks that the Prayer-Book itself seemed to share in his funeral, for on the same day, the Parliament made it a crime to use it in any solemnity whatever; and I endeavored to recall the scene of desolation which must then have smitten to the heart any true son of the Church of England who was its spectator, beholding, as he did, the Primate of all England going down into the sepulchre, as the last, apparently, of his dignity and order; the Church herself beheaded, if not destroyed, with him; and the Prayer-Book reading its own burial! Thank God, there I stood, two hundred years later, a living witness of the resurrection of that Church and its ritual, and of its powerful life, in the new world of the West."— [*Coxe's England*, page 81.]

that he might be buried within the walls of his own college, and this desire was, eventually, accomplished. After the troublesome times had passed, and the down-trodden Church had again lifted up her head from the dust, the Fellows of the College over which he had once presided, caused his remains to be removed to the chapel of St. John Baptist, at Oxford. This was on the 4th of July, 1663. There the ashes of Archbishop Laud were deposited beneath the altar, close by the bones of Sir Thomas Whyte, the munificent founder of the institution.

A traveller from our own land, who paid a visit to the spot, has made this touching note of it: "Going, quite alone, to St. John's College, I indulged myself in delightful meditations as I lounged in its gardens, and watched the young gownsmen shooting arrows at a target, or enjoying themselves about the walks. I went into the quadrangle, that munificent monument of Laud's affection for his beloved college. I passed on to the chapel. The door was not locked, and I entered it alone. Beneath the altar lies the Archbishop's mutilated corpse; and there, too, lies the stainless Juxon, whom he loved so well, and who served the last moments of Charles the First with the holy offices of the Church. I gave myself up to the powerful impressions of the spot, and spent a few minutes in very solemn meditations. In the library of the college I afterwards saw the pastoral crook of the martyred Primate, the little staff which supported his tottering steps on the scaffold, and the cap which covered his venerable head only a few minutes before it fell from the block." *

By his last will, Laud declared that he died a true and faithful member of the Protestant Church of England. His chief bequests are as follows:

First, — the sum of £800 towards the repair of St. Paul's, if that work should be continued. This sum, however, it would appear, had been already consigned to the custody of some trustee, with a view to its

* Impressions of England, page 138.

application to the purpose in question; for, he adds, "my executors are not charged with this. It is safe, in other hands."

Secondly, he leaves £1000 to the King, besides remitting to his Majesty a debt of £2000.

Thirdly, he bequeathes to St. John's College, his chapel plate, furniture, and books; together with £500 to be invested in the purchase of land; the rent of which was to be distributed every fourth year among the Fellows and scholars. "Something else," he says, with modest reference to his own princely benefactions, "I have done for them already, according to my ability. And God's everlasting blessing be upon that place, and that society, forever."

Then follow various smaller legacies to friends, servants, and others, amounting in all to about £1800. Among these bequests, is the sum of £100, for the purpose of translating his book against Fisher into Latin, "that the Christian world might see, and judge of his religion."

If these dispositions were carried into effect, it may be concluded, that, although his persecutors kept him from the use of his property during his imprisonment, they did not aggravate their infamy, by confiscating the remnants of it, after his death. His concluding words are, "Thus I forgive all the world; and heartily desire forgiveness of God and the world. And so, again, I commend and commit my soul into the hands of God the Father who gave it; in the merits and mercies of my blessed Saviour, Jesus Christ, who redeemed it; and in the peace and comfort of the Holy Ghost, who blessed it; and in the truth and unity of His Holy Catholic Church; and in the communion of the Church of England, as it yet stands established by law." From which solemn asseveration it follows, either that the heart of Archbishop Laud was faithful to the religion which he was accused of undermining; or else, that he was prepared to appear in the presence of God *with a lie in his right hand!*

And now, in bringing this painful chapter

to a close, we cannot do better than to adopt Robert Southey's striking words. "The enemies of Laud cut off from him, at the utmost, a few short years of infirmity and pain; and this was all they could do! They removed him from the sight of calamities, which would have been to him tenfold more grievous than death; and they afforded him an opportunity of displaying at his trial and on the scaffold, as in a public theatre, a presence of mind, a strength of intellect, a calm and composed temper, an heroic and saintly magnanimity, which he never could have been known to possess, if he had not thus been put to the proof. Had they contented themselves with stripping him of his rank and fortune, and letting him go to the grave a poor and broken-hearted old man, their calumnies might then have proved so effectual, that he would have been more noted now for his infirmities than for his great and eminent virtues. But they tried him in the burning fiery furnace of affliction, and so his sterling worth was assayed and proved. And the martyrdom of Cranmer is not more inexpiably disgraceful to the Papists than that of Laud to the Puritan persecutors."

CHAPTER NINETEENTH.

Outline of Character — Vandyck's Portrait — Personal Appearance of Laud — Dress — Mode of Living — Kindness to the Poor — Tenderness of Heart — His Faithful Servants — Scholarship — Habits of Prayer — Causes of his Unpopularity — His unfortunate Manners — A Conference with a Friend on this Subject — Too much of a Politician — Attachment for the King — Conclusion.

HAVING thus traced the remarkable career of Archbishop Laud to its close, it will be proper, in this chapter, to attempt something like an outline of his character.

But first, our younger readers especially, who are most curious in such matters, will be anxious to know what sort of a looking man he was. The portrait which adorns this volume is thought to be a good one, having been copied from a painting by Vandyck.*

* This most celebrated of all portrait-painters was born at Antwerp in 1598. He came to England after he had earned for himself a high reputation in other coun-

The Archbishop was low in stature, and the whole frame of his body rather diminutive. His eye was bright and piercing, and his countenance expressive both of gravity and quickness. He wore his hair so short, that one who did not know him might have supposed that he was a Roundhead.

He always dressed with the utmost simplicity and plainness, and no one could ever accuse him of wasting money for his own personal gratification, or for advancing the fortunes of his kindred. He never married, and his whole life was devoted to the interests of the Church. His diet was uniformly temperate, and his walk and conversation blameless. Archbishop Laud won the blessings of the poor by his many acts of kindness towards them, and his public benefactions for the encouragement of learning will preserve his memory for generations yet to come.

tries, at the invitation of Charles I., who bestowed many favors upon him, and dubbed him a Knight. Vandyck rewarded the King's generosity by increasing diligence, and he enriched England with his master-pieces, besides painting a great number of portraits. He died in 1641, and was buried in St. Paul's Church.

His tenderness of heart is discovered in numerous incidental references in his Diary. Thus, in one place, we find these words: "The way to do the town of Reading good for their poor, which may be compassed by God's blessing upon me, though my wealth be small. And I hope God will bless me in it, because it was his own motion in me. For this way never came into my thoughts (though I had much beaten them about it), till this night as I was at my prayers. Amen, Lord."

Again, we read concerning his faithful attendants: "October 2. Saturday, in the evening, at Mr. Windebank's, my ancient servant, Adam Torless, fell into a swoon, and we had much ado to recover him; but I thank God, we did."

"Thursday, September 23, 1641. Mr. Adam Torless, my ancient, loving, and faithful servant, and then my steward, after he had served me full forty and two years, died, to my great both loss and grief. For all my accounts since my commitment were in his hands; and had he not been a very honest and careful man, I must have suffered much more than I did; yet I suffered enough, besides the loss of his person, who was become almost the only comfort of my affliction and my age. So true it is, that afflictions seldom come single."

"October 26. Monday. This morning, between four and five of the clock, lying at Hampton Court, I dreamt that I was going out in haste, and that when I came into my outer chamber, there was my servant William Pennell, in the same riding-suit which he had on that day seven-night at Hampton Court with me. Methought I wondered to see him, for I left him sick at home, and asked him how he did, and what he made there. And that he answered me he came to receive my blessing; and with that fell on his knees. That thereupon I laid my hand upon his head and prayed over him, and therewith awaked. When I was up, I told this to them of my chamber, and added, that I should find Pennell dead or dying. My coach came, and when I came home I found him past sense, and giving up the ghost. So my prayers (as they had frequently before), commended him to God."

As a scholar, we have had occasion to speak of him before. He was no mean theologian, and while his style of writing is far from attractive, it certainly has the merit of being vigorous and pithy.

But better far than all mental gifts and stores of learning, it can be said of Laud, with strictest truth, that he was a man of prayer. The distractions of the times, the multiplicity of occupation, the troubles of his position, prevented not the communion of his soul with his heavenly Father. Seven times a day did he pour out his confessions, prayers, thanksgivings, at the throne of grace; nor were the dark and silent watches of the night unprovided in his manual with suitable devotions, the language of which is remarkably scriptural, and showed a mind deeply imbued with knowledge of Holy Writ. The same book contains special prayers for prosperity, for adversity, for the State, the King, the Church, the Clergy. His own failings are subject of particular note. The prayers for bridling of the tongue we have already alluded to, and we know the bitter penitential mournings each anniversary of his fall wrung from him. If the pestilence raged, or war broke out, or famine, Laud made it a subject of prayer. In poverty and sorrow and infamy, in fear of violence, of fraud, of treachery, the Prelate's soul vented its wants in prayer. His enemies were not forgotten, and the Saviour's precepts of forgiveness were embodied in the language of devotion.

With all these things in his favor, one not familiar with Laud's history might wonder what could have rendered him so extremely unpopular. We have before suggested some reasons for this in the course of our narrative.

He appears to have been peculiarly ungracious and forbidding in his manners, and it seems never to have occurred to him that a person can render himself much more useful by attending to the courtesies and civilities of life. In his history of his own Life, Clarendon gives an interesting account of a conference between himself and Laud, in 1635, in which the young lawyer did his best to open the eyes of his friend to this serious defect.

"He found the Archbishop, one morning early, in that part of his garden which to this day is known as Clarendon's Walk. He was graciously received; and asked what good news there was in the country. The answer of Hyde was, that there was no good news; that the people were universally discontented; and spoke of his Grace as the cause of all that was amiss. Laud replied, that he was sorry to hear this; but added, that he knew that he had done nothing to deserve the censure; and that he must not desist from serving the King and the Church in order to please the people. Hyde then told him, that there could be no necessity for an abatement of his zeal either for King or Church; but that it grieved him to find that many persons of the best condition, who were well affected to both, were, nevertheless, extremely ill disposed towards his Grace, and complained of the treatment they experienced from him, whenever they had occasion to resort to him. He then mentioned several instances, in illustration and support of this unwelcome remark. The Archbishop listened patiently to the recital; and his reply was abundantly mild and candid. But it showed that the defect was then inveterate and incurable. He said that he was very unfortunate to be so misunderstood; that, by nature, the tone of his voice was sharp, and might cause men to believe that he was angry, when it was no such thing; that with his pressing variety of occupations, he had no time to spare for compliments (for which, however, Richelieu contrived to find abundant leisure); that his integrity and uprightness would be found beyond reproach; and that, if these could not preserve him, he must even submit to God's pleasure. In spite of all this, Hyde still pressed him close; and wished that he would more restrain his passion towards all men, however faulty they might be; and particularly that he would treat persons of honor, and quality, and interest in the country, with more courtesy and condescension; especially when they came to visit him, and to make offer of their service. All, however, would not do. Laud was then sixty-two years of age; and at that period of life, any essential alteration of his manners was a hopeless matter. He replied, smiling, that he could only answer for his heart; that his meaning was good; that for his tongue, he could not undertake that he might not, sometimes, speak more hastily and sharply than he ought, (which oftentimes he was sorry for,) and that, consequently, he might be liable to misconstruction with those who knew not that such was his infirmity; and that it was so rooted in him by nature and education, that it was altogether vain to contend with it. He then adverted to the imputation of maintaining too stately a distance towards those who resorted to him; and intimated that really it was no more than was suitable to his rank in the Church and in the State. He then adverted to the behavior of that grave religionist, his predecessor, Archbishop Abbot, towards the greatest nobility of the realm; which, however, he allowed to have been, frequently, most insolent and inexcusable; and which, as Hyde observes, was, beyond all question, exceedingly ridiculous." *

Another cause of his unpopularity was the part which he took in political affairs. During the dark ages, when comparatively few could read or write, the Laity may have quietly yielded to the dominion of their Bishops, whether they acted in a civil or spiritual capacity, but in the days of Laud, England had many noble statesmen who could have attended to the concerns of government much better than he did. Moreover, it was hardly to be expected that one man could act as Prime Minister of that

* La Bas, page 333.

great nation, Foreign Secretary, and Chancellor of two Universities, besides discharging his duties of Archbishop of Canterbury, without making mistakes, and our only wonder is that they were not more numerous and glaring.

Laud loved Charles Stuart, and the wrong-doings of the King were visited upon him. Believing that the King would do all in his power to sustain the Church, he gladly threw the whole weight of his influence into the scale of monarchy, and thus he was brought into direct opposition to the Parliament, and the growing strength of Puritanism.

With all his faults, we must esteem him a good, well-meaning man, — one who did some unfortunate things, — but who showed how sincere he was in his principles by dying for them.

THE END.

www.ingramcontent.com/pod-product-compliance
Lightning Source LLC
LaVergne TN
LVHW010234110826
845151LV00004B/1294

* 9 7 8 1 4 2 5 5 2 5 2 3 1 *